MANA

MW01701667

BUILD TRUST

You don't need all the answers.
You just need the courage to lead with trust.

MANAGERS WHO BUILD TRUST
by Justin Patton

Copyright © 2025, Justin Patton. All rights reserved.
This book may not be reproduced in whole or in part without written permission from the author, except by a reviewer who may quote brief passages in a review; nor may any part of this book be reproduced, stored in a retrieval system, or transmitted in any form or by any means, including electronic, photocopying, recording, or other, without written permission from the author.

Printed in the United States of America
FIRST EDITION, SEPTEMBER 2025

Limit of Liability/Disclaimer of Warranty:
While the author has used his best efforts in preparing this book, he makes no representations or warranties with respect to the accuracy or completeness of the contents of this book, and specifically disclaims any implied warranties of merchantability or fitness for a particular purpose. The advice and strategies contained here may not be suitable for your situation. You should consult with a professional where appropriate. The author shall not be liable for any loss of profit or any other commercial damages, including but not limited to special, incidental, consequential, or other damages.

Managers Who Build Trust
Your Playbook for Bringing Out the Best in Your Team

978-1-7328766-7-5 (paperback)
979-8-9901329-3-1 (ebook)
979-8-9901329-4-8 (audiobook)

Written by Justin Patton
Designed by Shaina Nielson

DEDICATION

In Memory of
DR. MARK GOULSTON

You taught me and so many others how to show up at our best, deeply listen, and lead ourselves and others better. You remind every manager that their presence is the greatest tool they have in bringing out the best in others. May your books and memory continue to be a guiding light for us all.

WHO SHOULD READ THIS BOOK

NEW OR ASPIRING MANAGERS

This book is for anyone who wants to go into management, or who is a new manager and wants practical tips on how to bring out the best in their team and the organization.

EXPERIENCED MANAGERS

If you're like me, sometimes you just need some different perspectives to get you moving in a better direction. This book will help you do that. For some of you, maybe you're struggling with a particular scenario right now. Hang in there. Management is hard sometimes, and I believe this book will help you refocus and choose a path forward.

LEADERSHIP PROGRAMS / COHORTS

My hope is that this mini-book becomes an essential resource in every company's leadership development program. These concepts are how I believe we can transform company culture, the employees' experience, and hopefully the level of service customers receive.

START HERE
TAKE THE TRUST AUDIT™

Before you dive into the plays in this book, start with a quick gut check.

The **Trust Audit™** is a **free**, 5-minute self-assessment that gives you a personalized score across the four core areas of building trust:

- Trust in Yourself
- Trust with Others
- Repairing Trust After It's Broken
- Preventing Trust Leaks Before They Turn Into Deficits

Your team already knows how safe — or unsafe — they feel. This audit helps you catch up.

Use your score to lead smarter, fix blind spots faster, and build trust that sticks.

TAKE THE TRUST AUDIT™ NOW AT MYTRUSTAUDIT.COM

TABLE OF CONTENTS

ONE

Management Sucks, but It Also Changes Lives

TWO

The Most Common Management Mistake

THREE

The Playbook for Managers Who Build Trust

FOUR

Play 1: Build Authentic Relationships

FIVE

Play 2: Set Clear Expectations

SIX

Play 3: Lean into Performance Conversations

SEVEN

Play 4: Recognize What's Right

EIGHT

Final Thoughts

NINE

Trust Manifesto

ONE

Does how you show up
Inspire others to want
To do more, be more?

MANAGEMENT SUCKS, BUT IT ALSO CHANGES LIVES

Here's the nitty-gritty truth: **Management sucks sometimes!** No one told you that when you applied for the role, did they? That's because we sell people on the "sexy" parts of management: leading a team, making more money, having more influence, and moving up in your career. They left out that the role often requires you to slow down in a world consumed by productivity, to give relevant feedback, to engage in difficult conversations, to hire and fire people, and to compete for limited resources. There will be days in management when you disappoint people, when you spend more time managing relationships than doing quantifiable work, and when you wish you would've handled situations better. Sounds exhausting, right?

So you might ask yourself: Why even go into management?

Management changes lives. There will be more invigorating days than those that suck, and these are the moments you must remember. When performed well, your role as a manager serves in three distinctive ways: 1) it inspires others to be better versions of themselves, 2) it teaches others how to work toward something collaboratively, and 3) it gives people opportunities to change the direction of their lives. Management is the highest form of service in any organization. It's not easy, but that's why it's so impactful.

Being a manager who builds trust will require you to show up differently than you have in the past. Whether you're a new manager, an experienced leader looking to hone their skills, or part of a leadership program, my hope is that this book will serve as your playbook for how to bring out the best in your team. I understand that no one book will give you everything you need to know about management. There is no one-size-fits-all approach to leadership or management. Nothing can prepare you for everything you'll experience, but this book can give you one heck of a jumpstart to managing effectively, bringing out the best in others, and creating a culture of trust that keeps people coming back for more. If that's what you want, then this book is for you!

IT'S ALL ABOUT TRUST

If you want to create the greatest impact possible in your organization, you must bring out the best in your people. Your efforts will be viewed through the filter of one simple fact: **If the way you lead and manage isn't building trust with others, it's not effective.** Your leadership presence should always be earning the confidence and trust of those around you.

I started The Trust Architect Group because trust doesn't just happen. It must be designed and purposefully built. I wanted to help leaders build communities where trust is present. **Managers are the most important trust architects in any organization.** Have you ever thought of yourself as a trust architect? You are. How you show up and lead others significantly influences whether people buy into your management style, the organization's direction, how people collaborate, and what people believe about themselves and their future inside the company. Every choice you make as a manager either builds or erodes trust, ultimately shaping the playbook for your team's success. That's the incredible responsibility you have inside your organization as a leader. **Leadership isn't about the title you hold but the trust you build.** Your management style should empower people to build trust in themselves and others. When that happens, you move the business forward, teams are more engaged, and your customers always receive a better experience.

The Harvard Business Review once published an article called "Connect, Then Lead," where they asked leaders, "Is it better to be loved or feared?" They defined love as possessing characteristics of warmth and trustworthiness, whereas fear is characterized as strength and competence. When asked why, they explained, "Most leaders today tend to emphasize their strength, competence, and credentials in the workplace, but that is exactly the wrong approach. Leaders who project strength before establishing trust run the risk of eliciting fear, and along with it a host of dysfunctional behaviors. Fear can undermine cognitive potential, creativity, and problem solving, and cause employees to get stuck and even disengage. A growing body of research suggests that the way to influence—and to lead—is to begin with warmth. Warmth is the conduit of influence."

I don't say this lightly: **Leading out of fear requires no talent.** Fear-based leadership is easy. Anyone can intimidate and bully people, and it will work for short-term results. People need their jobs and the financial security they bring. However, it'll never set you up for long-term success or make you the type of leader who leaves a positive legacy in people's lives, or garners respect. Leading through trust is harder. It takes time, intentionality, and consistent effort to prove to each other that you're in this together. Leaders focused on trust always play the long game, and that's better for every relationship and organization.

Influence is about making an impact, which isn't created through force or aggression. A manager who builds trust understands that influence is a subtle, nuanced approach to inspiring change in others. It's about using their presence to earn credibility, to demonstrate empathy, and to build trust so that individuals exceed their own expectations. **Managers who build trust understand they're more than just managers. They're catalysts for change, architects of culture, and champions of people and performance.** Their impact resonates beyond the bottom line; it echoes in the growth of the people they lead, the satisfaction of their clients, and the legacy they leave.

WHAT IS YOUR PRIMARY ROLE AS A MANAGER?

Your primary responsibility as a manager is to no longer do the work but to empower others to get the work done through a team effort. This will require a very different skillset than when you were an individual contributor. American businesswoman and *Shark Tank* star Barbara Corcoran once explained that the root of being a great boss is remembering the cardinal rule: "I work for you; you don't work for me." Seeing your team member as your customer is a mindset shift. Think about it: How would you show up if you gave your team the level of service you expected them to provide the company's customers? When you adopt that mindset, it changes your leadership approach for the better. You'll be more intentional about building relationships, celebrating your team, and giving the feedback and coaching they need to ensure everyone is set up for success.

Organizations often promote people to management who were very effective in their previous roles as individual contributors. The problem with this philosophy is that many high performers are solo artists. They excel at their jobs when left alone, but they're not always the best for collaborating. If you're reading or listening to this right now and thinking, *Oh no, that's me!* that's okay. I appreciate and respect your awareness! Let's now take it a step further: With that awareness you can now make some different choices.

Management isn't a solo act. Management is an orchestra, and you're the conductor. Everyone is relying on you to bring order and create music from what could be chaos by itself. There's an art to getting people to move and work together harmoniously. This will require excellent performances from every musician. It will also require the conductor to ensure the performers have the tools, resources, knowledge, and feedback to produce a memorable product that brings people back for more! On the good days, you'll get a standing ovation. On the bad ones, you'll question what the hell you're doing.

If you want to be successful—which I know you do because you picked up this book—the role of manager will challenge you to release control, meet people where they are, become a better communicator, and be a champion in people's lives. In doing so, you'll earn their commitment instead of just their compliance. You will also be able to move the business forward in a way that's a win-win for everyone.

Empowering others to get the work done through a team effort will require you to show up differently than you did in the past. If you utilize only a handful of the teachings from this book, I want you to have some actionable tactics for showing up differently. Here are four actions you can immediately implement to have a better leadership presence as a manager and create a quicker impact.

LEADERSHIP PLAYS FOR MAXIMUM IMPACT

1. Lead with Your Head And Heart.

In 2015, I was hiking through the five towns of Cinque Terre, Italy, with two good friends. We were having a great time admiring the views when they suddenly turned to me and said, "Justin, can we give you some feedback?" Now, y'all know nothing warm and fuzzy comes after the phrase, "Can we give you some feedback." However, I trusted these individuals and their friendship. I braced myself, then said, "Of course." They went on to share: "We feel in life we often get all of you or none of you, and we think the best version of you is somewhere in the middle." Wow! That took a minute to digest. But I realized they were right, and that insight helped me cultivate more self-awareness and lead myself and others better.

See, none of us show up at our best when we operate from an extreme version of either head or heart. When a manager only leads from their headspace, they often rely on their competence and intellectual abilities rather than considering emotions and the impact of their actions on interpersonal dynamics. As a result, they're usually seen as transactional, only focused on the bottom line. On the other hand, when you have a manager who only leads from their heart space, they often prioritize empathy and compassion above everything else. As a result, they sometimes don't hold people accountable, don't make decisions as quickly as they need, and lack the necessary strategic decision-making skills for long-term success.

Managers who build trust understand that emotional intelligence is the unique intersection of both head and heart, as Yale's David Caruso once stated. The delicate balancing of both qualities enables managers to drive exceptional results while making people feel exceptional in the process. Don't buy into the belief that you must sacrifice one for the other.

I once coached a female executive who stopped me in the middle of the session and said, "I realize now I was so afraid of being labeled a bitch that I became homecoming queen." We discussed that neither of those extremes served her team or the business. The best version of her was in the middle of those, and we explored what it would look like to lead from that middle.

I was once brought in to help a manager who needed to perform better. Trust had eroded with everyone around them, and they needed some help getting out of their own way. In my first session, I asked, "So tell me why I'm here." This individual had criticized their direct supervisor for not supporting them, even though their boss paid for the coaching because they saw this person's potential. They blamed the organization's president and didn't think that person knew how to do his job. Then they blamed everyone on their team for not being engaged and wasting time. Wow! I acknowledged that it sounded overwhelming and emotionally exhausting, but I also hoped they could be open to seeing the situation differently. I asked, "Can I share something my momma used to tell me?" They obliged. "My momma once told me, 'Baby, when everyone's the problem, you're the problem.'" We explored her role in the breakdown of her relationships and the results. She slowly started to make different choices once she asked herself, "What choices would I make if I was focused on building trust with others?"

Every person is hardwired to lead more from either their heart space or headspace. This is part of the value you bring to a team. However, managers who build trust spend their careers investing in emotional intelligence and learning how to lead with both their head and heart. The art of management is knowing when you need to flex your go-to style and lean in a different direction so you can bring out the best in others.

2. Establish Credibility as a Manager.

Your credibility as a manager will determine the level of buy-in you receive, and what doors open and close for you and your team. Establishing credibility requires managing the glimpses people always get of you, whether in person or virtually. Why? Because most people in life will never know you at the level of your family or best friend. Most people in your organization will only get glimpses of you throughout the day, weeks, or months! And based on those glimpses, they'll decide if they trust you, if you're someone they want to work with more, and if you demonstrate all the things you say you really value. Every decision you make as a manager now impacts you, your team, and the organization. You don't get an off day, which isn't easy because you'll mess up occasionally. But you must get it right most of the time.

Sound exhausting? It is, because it requires you to be intentional and take complete responsibility for your energy. Pat Summitt, one of the most successful NCAA basketball coaches of all time, said it best: "You can't pick and choose the days that you feel like being responsible. It's not something that disappears when you're tired."

Your credibility is based on three foundational factors:

- Image
- Competence
- Character

Managers who build trust understand the effect of these three factors on their credibility, and they do their best to manage the glimpses seen in each area.

Image

According to research from the Center for Talent Innovation, appearance is five percent of someone's total leadership presence. Now, that number might seem low, but don't discount the power of its impact. The research says you must get past this five percent to get through the door to the other credibility factors. Image is situational. You must look like you fit in with that group of people you're with. For example, I'm currently coaching an executive who's been given feedback that their appearance lacks the polish the board expects from their executives. This doesn't require the executive to give up their personal style or identity. They simply need to understand the overall style within the work culture, then determine how they can best adapt while remaining professional yet distinctive. My philosophy is that people should not be so distracted by your appearance that they can't hear your message. If this happens, you damage your credibility.

Competence

Competence is about what you know. People need to believe you know what you're talking about. You have an obligation to yourself and your team to stay on top of trends in your company and within your specific industry.

Early in my career, I had coffee with a mentor from Fifth Third Bank. During our conversation, he asked me, "What do you want to be an expert in?" No one had ever asked me that question before. He added, "You might not be an expert today, but what do you want to be the go-to expert for in the future?" That question opened me up to a new world of possibility and development. Once I got clear on my answer, I went all-in on developing myself through books, seminars, certifications, and then living it out. Becoming an expert in an area gives you a point of view that many others won't have in the spaces you're in. That differentiates you. That becomes part of the value you bring every day.

Another way you can grow your competence and highlight the expertise of people on your team is by giving one member in every meeting a space to share their brilliance. Maybe they share an article they found valuable, lead a discussion on a current topic in the industry, or highlight their top three to five lessons everyone in this industry should know. The best managers don't have to know all the information, but they do create space for others to learn from each other.

Character

Character is how you act. I'm not as concerned about how you act when you feel good and everything's going well. It's easy to show up at our best in these moments. I want to see how you act when people don't meet your expectations. How do you show up when you're frustrated? Does your presence help keep everyone else calm and moving forward? Are people following you because they have to, or do they follow you because they believe in your leadership?

When I ask individuals to think of the most effective manager of their career, they always talk about leaders whose character they admire. They'll say they were supportive, trustful, a good listener, honest, or someone who gave them autonomy. Rarely do they talk about how bright or clever the person was. Managers with strong character always help others believe in themselves; as a result, others believe in them.

Hear me when I tell you this: Image and competence will get you in the door. Character is what allows you to stay. Let me prove it to you. Think about celebrities who were highly competent in their field/industry, but who sabotaged their careers because they didn't take responsibility for their character. Who comes to mind? People often say names like Matt Lauer, Paula Deen, Lance Armstrong, Charlie Sheen, Ellen

DeGeneres, Chris Brown, Will Smith, or Lindsay Lohan (even though I'm still rooting for her comeback).

Their character, not their competence, derailed their career and success. Don't get me wrong; competence is important. It's one of the first building blocks for you to earn credibility. But your character will ultimately shape your team's culture and your legacy as a manager.

3. Create a Culture That Brings out People's Best.

I've said it before, and I'll keep reiterating it: **Organizations thrive or die based on the quality of their managers.** That's because, as a manager, you have the most significant impact on an associate's day-to-day experience, and the most influence on whether your organization retains or loses its talent. In a 2021 SHRM Omnibus Survey, one of the key findings was that "fifty-three percent of Americans who left a job due to workplace culture report leaving because of their relationship with their manager." I suspect we'll continue to see this trend.

Executives help create the vision for the culture, but managers are the ones who ensure the culture is lived out daily. Managers who build trust understand the recklessness of letting culture "just happen." Therefore they take a proactive approach in holding themselves and others accountable for creating a space where people feel they belong and want to come back again and again.

So, let's get into a few principles you should know about workplace culture as a manager who builds trust.

First, culture is developed by which consistent behaviors get rewarded in an organization. People know what they can and cannot get away with, so most always rise to whatever level of accountability and recognition they receive. I'm not concerned about the values you post on your company walls or website. That's lip service! I want to watch how your people treat each other in meetings. I want to see if your performance reviews measure people living these stated values day to day. I want people promoted who are the best culture champions in the organization, and I want to see how the recognition inside the company ties back to the core values the company says it stands for every day. Show me what you reward, and I'll show you what you really value.

Second, a great team culture requires psychological safety. Dr. Amy Edmonson defined psychological safety as "a belief that I will not be punished or humiliated for speaking up with ideas, questions, concerns, or mistakes." As a manager, you're in the safety business. When your team knows you'll lead that way, you signal that authenticity, candor, and risk-taking are not just welcome but expected. Safety is the foundation for how trust is built, and it must be one of your top priorities as a manager who builds trust.

In my book on how to build trust, *Your Road to Yes!*, I share **ten actions all leaders can take to create psychological safety on a team:**

1. Check in regularly
2. Encourage idea sharing
3. Invite and give feedback
4. Squash judgment
5. Admit mistakes
6. Ask questions
7. Show empathy
8. Champion diversity
9. Assign team collaborations
10. Reward candor

Third, your high performers are wild horses who need to run. Let them run! Give them the autonomy to find new paths. Allow them to take calculated risks. Praise them for challenging your current way of thinking. The worst thing a manager can do is hold the reins too tight and try to keep their team members confined to a space too small for their potential. Passion and creativity will never stay contained for long. It always finds a way to break free. That doesn't mean you just let them run however they want. Even wild horses need someone to ride beside them. The best managers encourage their high performers to run while giving them the feedback they need to run successfully in their organization. They slowly guide them on how to help lead the herd, not go at everything alone. Their wild spirit is their gift to the organization, and managers who build trust help guide that spirit in a direction that serves everyone.

Finally, rebel against toxic workplace behaviors. *MIT Sloan Management Review* published an article in 2022 called "Why Every Leader Needs to Worry About Toxic Culture." Their research reinforced what we've seen time and time again: Toxic culture is one of the most significant factors in why employees leave their jobs. Specifically, their research found that "a toxic corporate culture was the single best predictor of attrition during the first six months of the Great Resignation—ten times more powerful than how employees viewed their compensation in predicting employee turnover." The research team went on to study more than 1.3 million Glassdoor reviews from U.S. employees of Culture 500 companies in an attempt to understand the patterns of toxic workplace cultures. MIT narrowed toxic culture down to five distinct attributes:

1. Disrespectful
2. Noninclusive
3. Unethical
4. Cutthroat
5. Abusive

No one, and I mean no one, wants to work in an environment where these five attributes are their day-to-day experience. It's exhausting and it's lonely. And let me be clear: it only takes one person who's consistently allowed to get away with bad behavior to disrupt the entire team dynamic and make it miserable for everyone else. Left unchecked, the culture of your team will slowly and methodically erode, trust will disintegrate, and people will focus more on self-preservation than on working together. You can't afford that, because trying to turn that ship around is hard. Your high performers will often jump ship before you've had time to course-correct, or you'll be tossed overboard and a new captain will take the lead.

I don't tell you this to scare you or make things seem bleak. My intent is to encourage you to hold people accountable for how they get results so that you never have to worry about a toxic workplace culture in the first place. Rebel against toxic workplace behaviors. Your team is relying on you.

4. Make Your Conversations Count.

Your ability to deliver on leading with head and heart, establishing credibility, and creating a culture that brings out people's best will all depend on your ability to make your conversations count. This is more than just your face-to-face communications; it includes your email responses, how you show up on social media, how you interact at outside work functions, and even your silence. Every conversation you have will either build or erode people's perception of your ability to lead others and make a positive impact.

Here are a few tips on how to make your conversations count as a manager, starting today.

Put Empathy Before Information

People will always be in a better place to hear you when they feel you care. Empathy is seeing beyond yourself and genuinely acknowledging someone else's experience. It doesn't require you to agree with their stance; it simply requires you to show up, hold space for that person, and really understand why they have that stance. My rule of thumb is always to demonstrate empathy when someone is communicating with a lot of intense emotion. They're signaling that they need to be acknowledged for what they're experiencing.

You make people feel seen when you articulate the emotion you think they're feeling and go deeper into why you think they're feeling that emotion. For example, you can say, "That must've been overwhelming. Not only did you have to figure out what you were going to do, but you also had to think about how to help your family at the same time. Sounds like everyone's expecting you to be a world-class juggler, but they're not understanding the impact that has on you."

You'll know you've created empathy when the person either nods or says, "Yes." You'll often see their posture relax and their intensity mellow. When this happens, they're better positioned to hear whatever comes next. And here's the good news: even if you don't get the emotion correct, you're giving them a chance to tell you their emotion, which means they'll still feel connected.

Frame Your Message as a Team Player

You won't always agree with every decision your company's leadership team makes, or every position of your peers. You're going to have moments where you're asked for an opinion, and it might be contrary to the majority in the room. When that happens, I want you to consider a few things.

Is this the hill you want to die on? I once had a boss who told me I had a strong opinion about everything; therefore it sometimes caused me to come across as the boy who cried wolf. Eventually, she warned me that people would simply stop listening to my opinions. She believed in me and thought I had great ideas, but she also wanted me to time and position them so that others could hear them. I now ask myself, "If I stay silent, will I still be able to be as kind and loving, or will I become resentful and pull back?" If it's something I can get over, then I'm okay with being silent. If I'm going to regret it and be tempted to pull back from a person, the leadership team, or the company, then I know it's my hill to die on, so I will speak up. There will be moments when you need to stand on that hill and accept the consequences of that choice, but not every hill is one of these.

Are you a team player? If so, how you position your thoughts should come across that way. I've spent years studying trust. What I know for sure is that transparency, tact, and togetherness are foundational factors when communicating. Trust requires all three. When you're transparent but lack togetherness, you come across as only looking out for yourself and/or your team. You'll often alienate others when this happens. It's possible to stay true to your beliefs while still making it feel like we're all in this together. That's communicating with impact.

Let me give you an example: An executive leadership team is considering changing the bonus structure for some of their staff, and you disagree with the approach.

> ***Response 1:*** "One thing I've always admired about our company is our commitment to do right by our people. I'm struggling because, based on what I just heard, it feels like this decision goes directly against that. If that's the case,

I would suggest we reevaluate the decision. However, maybe there's something I'm not seeing. Can you help me understand?"

Response 2: "This is ridiculous! You say you care about people, and then you make policies that go directly against that. This isn't the right approach, and it'll lead to nothing but disaster."

There will be people out there who resonate more with the second response. I get it. It's assertive and the type of language we often see in movies and television shows. But it lacks tact. It's not only judgmental, but uses deliberately intense language to shut down the conversation. Nothing about this comment invites collaboration, curiosity, or further understanding. You also see the pronoun choice of "you" more in this communication style. Frequent communication like this will exhaust others and cause them to pull back from you.

The first response also conveys that the speaker doesn't agree with the decision based on what they heard, but they anchored it to a statement that everyone at the meeting can agree with. You see more pronouns of "I" and "us" being used, which makes it feel less hostile. Additionally, they asked a question at the end that invited more conversation. This demonstrates openness and that you're willing to figure this out together.

Vent in Private; Lead in Public

In my previous book, *Leadership Presence*, I shared that you have every right to process and express your feelings. In fact, being able to name and understand your feelings is a healthy sign of emotional intelligence. However, do it privately with people who've earned the right to hear it.

When you vent your unexamined feelings in the public domain, especially in front of people with little to no context of who you are, you're allowing intensity to get in your way. It comes across as professional immaturity. You may feel better after calling others out. It might make for a good episode of a reality television show. You might even intimidate others from speaking up and challenging you. But those outcomes cost you trust and credibility. It's always a lose-lose scenario.

Leading in public doesn't mean you never show emotion. Instead, it means expressing your thoughts without being emotional in the process. Leadership presence requires you to be aware of your delivery and ensure that this delivery builds trust with your audience. You erode trust when people talk more about your delivery than your message.

Be Brief and Brilliant

Work to be brief and brilliant when sharing your ideas in a meeting. Too many people keep talking past their point and thus weaken their message. Share your perspective and why you believe what you do. Once you make a solid point and reach that sentence's period, stop.

You now know your primary responsibility as a manager who builds trust. You've learned a few actions to help you earn credibility and make a bigger impact. In the next chapter, we will explore the biggest management mistake I see leaders make so that it never becomes your story.

CHAPTER SUMMARY

- Being a manager who builds trust will require you to show up differently than you have in the past.
- Your primary responsibility as a manager is to no longer do the work, but to empower others to get the work done through a team effort.
- Being a manager who builds trust will require you to lead with a balance of both head and heart qualities.
- Leadership isn't about the title you hold; it's about the trust you build. If the way you lead and manage isn't building trust with others, it's not effective.
- Managers who build trust understand they're more than just managers. They're catalysts for change, architects of culture, and champions of people and performance.
- Culture is developed by which consistent behaviors get rewarded in an organization.
- A great team culture requires psychological safety.
- Establishing credibility requires you to manage the glimpses that people get of you at all times.
- Your credibility is based on three foundational factors: image, competence, and character.
- Image and competence will get you in the door. Character is what allows you to stay.

TAKE THE TRUST AUDIT™ NOW AT MYTRUSTAUDIT.COM

TWO

A hands-off approach
Is never the way to go.
Teams deserve better.

THE BIGGEST MANAGEMENT MISTAKE

It doesn't matter what title your manager holds—people leader, boss, coach, team lead, or supervisor. Each manager has the same crucial responsibility: to empower their team and drive the organization forward. But if that's not happening, it's time to call it out for what it is: undermanagement. Undermanagement is far too common, and it's hurting organizations everywhere.

Undermanagement refers to a lack of direction or guidance from a leader. It involves taking a hands-off approach and failing to provide the necessary clarity and support for team members to succeed in their roles. Undermanagement leads to confusion, misalignment of resources, and poor performance.

There's a clear reason why undermanagement happens so frequently. We're promoting people into positions without giving them the resources they need to be successful. Too many organizations are leaving managers to figure it out on their own. I'm all for some on-the-job learning, but it shouldn't be a sink-or-swim mentality. A 2020 study from the Society of Human Resource Management found that 84 percent of US workers say poorly trained managers created a lot of unnecessary work and stress.

Managers Aren't Trained and Ready

Traci was a store manager for a large restaurant franchise and had been deemed a "high performer" six months earlier, which led to more and more work being assigned to her. One day she received a call from her direct supervisor, asking if she could come to the restaurant a bit earlier than normal. When she arrived, she found not only her manager, but the human resource manager, who told her they wanted to discuss her lack of performance. They proceeded to put her on a performance improvement plan. Traci was blindsided. Her manager had had no previous conversations about her performance and had never given any indications before now that it needed to improve. Needless to say, Traci's trust in her leader was almost entirely destroyed in just one act of bad management. Not surprisingly, before the month was over, Traci quit and found herself a new job. Everyone lost in this situation.

I've talked with several people in healthcare who say they constantly feel penalized for being a high performer. Their managers rely so heavily on them because they know they'll get the work done, which leads to them continuing to pile on more responsibility while allowing other employees to coast. One person said to me, "I'm drowning in the hospital while others are chilling in the breakroom. It's easier for management to ask me to do something because they know I will, versus holding others accountable. I really wish they would just hold everyone accountable." It's this unresolved frustration that often leads a high-performing employee to burnout.

I can confidently say after coaching countless mid-level managers to executives for the past decade that **most organizational problems are a result of undermanagement.**

SIX WARNING SIGNS OF UNDERMANAGEMENT

You might be wondering how you can detect undermanagement in your organization, or if you're being undermanaged. Below are six warning signs of undermanagement.

1. Lack of Self-Confidence

A lack of authentic confidence will hold you back as a leader. What you believe or don't believe about yourself drives your actions. When you lack belief in yourself, you typically don't speak up when you should, you're hesitant to take risks, you outsource your decision-making and become overly reliant on the opinion of others, and you fail to communicate effectively. A lack of self-confidence is the catalyst for the other undermanagement warning signs.

2. Poor Communication

Leaders who undermanage don't effectively communicate with their team, don't provide the feedback people need to grow and don't have the difficult conversations necessary for a successful outcome. They often replace transparency with silence, and then trust is eroded because people feel they're left in the dark.

3. Putting Empathy over Accountability

Leaders who undermanage often use empathy as a badge of honor for being liked and loved, but it then becomes an excuse for not holding people accountable.

4. Not Having Consistent One-on-Ones

Leaders who undermanage are so busy being busy that they prioritize everything else over their one-on-ones with their team members. As a result, they fail in numerous ways: getting to know their people outside of the day-to-day work environment, updating them on team and organization changes, aligning on work so everyone knows how their tasks impact each other, or having the confidential space to give the feedback needed to grow.

5. Taking on Work That Is Not Their Responsibility

Leaders who undermanage often relinquish responsibility from team members and start taking on work they shouldn't. They'll justify their actions with excuses like, "It'll just be quicker if I do it." In the desire to appear as a strong leader who will "jump in there with the team," they fail to delegate and then often complain about their workload.

6. Being Too Concerned with Being Liked

Leaders who undermanage are often well-liked by their team because they provide extreme autonomy. Unfortunately, this can lead to difficulty in making decisions that aren't popular, and a failure to address problems. Leadership isn't always comfortable, and being "liked" isn't always possible in every moment. You owe it to yourself, to the other person, and to the organization to be uncomfortable when necessary.

While one warning sign of undermanagement doesn't necessarily mean a leader is underperforming, it's a safe bet that something may be off when multiple signs are present. Keep an eye out for these warning signs to ensure your team is receiving the guidance and support it needs to succeed.

Your Part In Combatting Undermanagement

It's time to take action against undermanagement in your organization. No matter your role, you can be part of the solution. Here are some steps to combat undermanagement and create a more positive and productive work environment.

Individual Contributors

Many managers are thrown into their roles without proper training or resources. But that doesn't mean you should just accept it. Instead, try collaborating with your manager and seeking their advice when it's appropriate. Rather than simply telling them you don't know what to do or what's expected of you, approach them with curiosity, and ask for their thoughts on a specific issue or project. For example: "I've been thinking about the next move on this project and wanted to get your thoughts to see if it makes sense." This type of proactive, collaborative approach can help your manager provide the clarity you need, which results in a win-win for both of you.

Managers

As a manager, it's important to take charge of your professional development. Consider investing in emotional intelligence training to improve your self-awareness and people skills. You could also create a peer mentor or mastermind group where you can regularly discuss challenges, gain insights, and set goals with your peers. Additionally, try asking your direct reports open-ended questions to get their perspectives.

Executive Leaders

As an executive leader, it's your responsibility to invest in the strategic development of your managers. This could involve providing formal training, offering mentorship opportunities, facilitating critical experiences, and gathering feedback through engagement surveys. It's essential that this development aligns with the values of your organization, and that managers are recognized and promoted for driving results while exemplifying those values. Investing in your managers sets your company apart from the competition, setting the stage for future success.

Managers are the lifeline of every business. Not only do they directly impact employee satisfaction and retention, they can also set the tone for the entire organization. Undermanagement can spell disaster for both managers and their teams, leading to long-term failure. By taking a proactive approach to addressing undermanagement and building a culture of transparency, support, and accountability, leaders can empower their team. This should always be the goal.

LEADING VS. ROWING THE BOAT

You can lead the boat or you can row the boat, but you cannot do both at the same time. And that's because you lead on the level of your perspective. Managers who build trust accept that there is a time to lead the boat and a time to row the boat, and they have the discernment to know which part to play at the right time.

Combating undermanagment requires you to show up and consistently deliver when it's your time to lead the boat. Leading the boat requires you to stand with the people who are rowing, but to also have the discernment to zoom out and see what they cannot see, anticipate what they cannot anticipate, and ensure they are set up for success.

More specifically, leading the boat requires you to:

- Discuss and align your crew with a vision.
- Ensure your team has the resources and knowledge to accomplish this vision.
- Remove any obstacles as quickly as possible.
- Recognize the team's efforts.
- Provide ongoing feedback and coaching to maximize performance.
- Knock anyone out of the boat who tries to sink it.

Rowing the boat requires you to:

- Buy into the vision that has been established.
- Focus on how *you* are rowing.
- Be open to feedback and coaching.
- Prove that you're a great team player.
- Contribute to the bigger picture.

High-performing teams understand the differences in these roles, and they honor each person for the part they play in contributing to the overall success of the team. Every team needs someone leading the boat and other people rowing. Dysfunction happens the moment everyone on a team is rowing or when multiple people are trying to lead the boat in different directions.

There are going to be times in management when you find yourself busy-being-busy, and you'll catch yourself rowing more than you're leading. This is usually what drives managers and their teams off course, which is how undermanagement happens. If you find yourself in this space, simply pause and decide what you need to do to get back to leading the boat in the right direction. Your crew is relying on you for many things: To ensure the culture inside the boat brings out the best in everyone. To make people feel valued for their contributions. To affirm when they are headed in a meaningful direction. The goal is to never drift for too long but to row with purpose and ensure people aren't ready to jump ship when they get to the destination. That is your responsibility. It's not easy, but it is rewarding.

Enjoy the journey!

CHAPTER SUMMARY

- Most organizational problems are a result of undermanagement.
- Undermanagement refers to a lack of direction or guidance from a leader.
- Undermanagement involves taking a hands-off approach and failing to provide the necessary clarity and support for team members to succeed in their roles.
- Undermanagement leads to confusion, misalignment of resources, and poor performance.
- The six warning signs of undermanagement include:
    1. Lack of self-confidence
    2. Poor communication
    3. Putting empathy over accountability
    4. Not having consistent one-on-ones
    5. Taking on work that is not your responsibility
    6. Being too concerned with being liked
- You can lead the boat or you can row the boat, but you cannot do both at the same time. And that's because you lead on the level of your perspective.

THREE

Bring out people's best
And work to a common goal.
That's transformative.

THE PLAYBOOK FOR MANAGERS WHO BUILD TRUST

One of my earliest and most influential introductions into effective management was from reality TV star Jo Frost. Stay with me! Frost is a global parenting expert for those who don't know. Her show, *Supernanny*, aired in the United States from 2005 through 2011, during the early formative years of my professional career. I'd watch her go into strangers' homes and positively disrupt their families. She would use her presence and expertise to get everyone on the same page and moving in the same direction. Time after time, I watched her bring out the best in others and help them imagine a life they didn't even know was possible. And isn't that what effective management is all about?

Being a manager who builds trust is all about our ability to bring out people's best as they work towards a common goal, and Jo Frost was one of my first role-modeled examples of transformative leadership in action.

As I started leading people and large projects in my career, I often thought of Jo Frost and the television show I watched for many years. When I analyzed what she did differently than so many other leaders, I realized something important: she consistently demonstrated specific habits that allowed her to create meaningful change and impact.

First, Frost consistently built authentic relationships. She was genuine, present, and focused on mutual respect. After forming a foundational relationship, she then set clear expectations so everyone played by the same rules. She understood that trust doesn't leave people second-guessing. We all show up better when we're clear on the boundaries and limits. Afterward, she would give *direct and safe* feedback to both the kids and parents. She found pivotal coaching moments to let people develop their own answers or practice a skill. Finally, she always made the time to recognize effort and constructive behaviors. She knew creating a positive reinforcement culture would lead to long-term sustainability and success. In her book, *Supernanny: How to Get the Best from Your Children*, she states, "Don't be stingy with praise."

My entire framework for managers who build trust was created based on what I observed from Supernanny Jo Frost, the interactions I've had with great leaders over the years, the successes and failures I've accumulated when managing others, and copious research on management and building a strong workplace culture. Based on what I've learned, I believe great leaders bring out the best in others when they consistently demonstrate the following four plays:

1. Build authentic relationships
2. Set clear expectations
3. Lean into performance conversations
4. Recognize what's right

I've spent more than a decade now coaching and teaching leaders, from mid-level managers to C-level executives. I've used these four plays of management successfully with college athletic directors, district managers running multimillion-dollar restaurants, and chamber of commerce leaders, among dozens of other professions. If these principles can work for them, I know they can work for you too.

Here's the good news: you don't have to be perfect at applying all four plays. That will take time and practice. However, your intentionality will go a long way with your team. And in a world where so many people don't feel seen and supported by their direct supervisor, you'll stand out. More importantly, you'll change what they believe about the role of managers and help them reimagine what's possible in their life, on their team, and in the company.

Let's explore the four plays for being a manager who builds trust and the antidote to undermanagement.

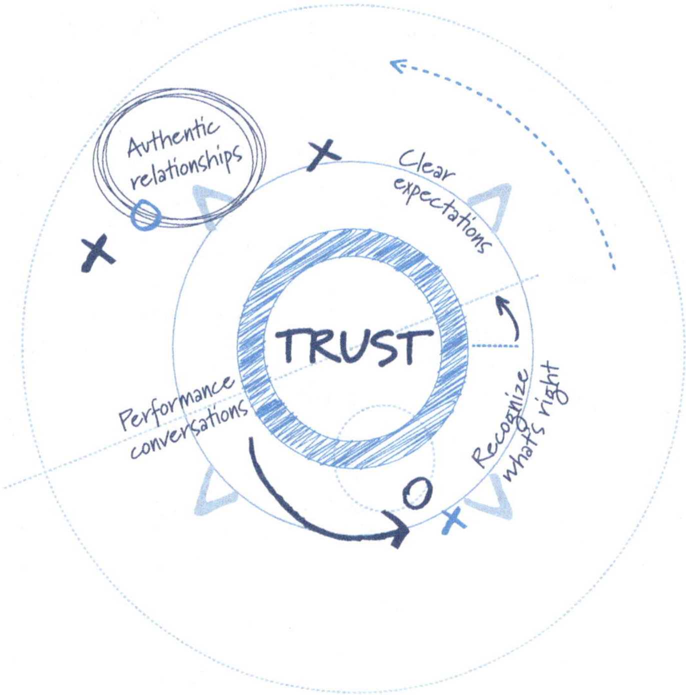

FOUR

Undeniable:
Leadership is about both
People and results.

PLAY 1: BUILD AUTHENTIC RELATIONSHIPS

Management is all about people and performance. Managers don't have the luxury of focusing only on one of those foundational factors. How a manager leads people and improves performance dictates their legacy, and it sets the tone for how engaged their team will be in the workplace.

There are two fundamentally different types of management mindsets. One is where managers sacrifice people to get results at any cost, and the other is where managers believe that results will come through taking care of their people. Both mindsets value results; they just have different philosophies on how to achieve these results. But let me be clear: **You can value excellence and results while still putting people first.** Managers who build trust always do.

Henry Ford once said, "A business that makes nothing but money is a poor business." Ford knew the hollowness of a financially rich but morally bankrupt organization. A company's long-term success must be built on more than just profit. Managers inside organizations have a responsibility to generate results, but they can do that while also building meaningful relationships, taking care of their communities, leaving the planet in a better place, and making a positive impact on the customers they serve.

One of the most important first steps you need to take as a manager who builds trust is building relationship capital across the organization. Doing so will help you earn trust and gain the necessary influence to drive awareness and change. Additionally, there will come a day when you'll need to cash in some of the relationship equity you built up. Please don't wait until there's an issue before you start focusing on building relationships.

Building meaningful relationships will require you to master the art of consistently showing up for yourself and others. There is no universal formula, but there are tactics I will share that I believe make a significant difference.

BUILDING THE RELATIONSHIP WITH YOURSELF

It's important that you first build an authentic relationship with yourself before you find yourself leading others. When we don't do that necessary work, we often use others to make ourselves feel successful, worthy, and seen. It ends up being exhausting for everyone.

My first book, *Bold New You*, is all about how to be a better leader of yourself. I wrote that book because a lot of us, myself included, found ourselves in management positions without ever doing the necessary soul-searching work we needed to do on ourselves. As I put it in that book:

Millions of people get up every morning and look in the mirror at a person they no longer recognize. They do not feel successful because they are not where they believe they should be on their journey. They condemn themselves for their past choices and rather than sit in the messiness of their life and do their work to heal, they protect themselves by emotionally disconnecting and making excuses for their behavior. As a result, they look in the mirror less and less. When we stop looking at the truth of our own reflection, we don't hold ourselves accountable to our own greatness and we act in ways that are incongruent with our best self.

Let me be clear: **you can't be a manager who builds trust and emotionally disconnected at the same time.** If you're going to show up for yourself, then you need to demonstrate five actions consistently:

1. Honor who you are at your best.

I've spoken to thousands of leaders around the world. I've never had one of them say, "At my best, I'm arrogant, condescending, and overbearing." But if you ask their team, they'll tell you this manager often shows up in these ways. That's because they forgot who they are, and walked away from their highest, best self. **Managers who build trust know who they are at their best and work hard to ensure their actions align with that vision.**

Recall a time in your life when you feel you consistently offered your best (personally or professionally), or a specific time you're proud of where you showed up in the moment. It could be reading a bedtime story to your kiddo, supporting your best friend during a really tough moment, giving a presentation and getting through it, working hard on a project, or overcoming a personally challenging situation.

Next, identify the top three actions you demonstrated that allowed you to show up at your best. Some common answers include confidence, empathy, being present, strategy, commitment, pride, patience, or kindness. What are your top three actions? You'll know you've picked the right actions when you can look back at yourself both personally and professionally and recognize that when you're at your best, it's because you're generally showing up that way.

Your answer is at the heart of authentic leadership. Everyone's core actions will be different. That's great. Again, there's no universal blueprint for leadership. Your job is not to be like everyone else, but to show up and consistently live out your authentic best.

There will be moments when you walk out of the truth of who you are even when you're at your best. But without a vision of who you are at your best, you won't be able to know you've walked away. We don't have to beat ourselves up when that happens though. What we must do is come back home to ourselves.

2. Develop authentic confidence.

The root of almost every problem I've ever coached people through is a lack of confidence. That lack of confidence can manifest as being a people-pleaser, being overly empathetic, or not holding people accountable. However, it can also disguise itself as being overly confident, being judgmental, and not being open to others' ideas.

I find that authentic confidence is often quiet and humble. It doesn't feel the need to boast or brag. Confident people aren't trying to prove they belong. They already believe they do. They're not caught up with trying to be the smartest person in the room. They recognize the value they bring into a space, and that's enough for them.

Confidence is the ability to let yourself be seen. And it requires two things: authenticity and vulnerability. Authenticity is a deep knowing of who you are. That's important because what we believe about ourselves becomes the filter for how we make decisions, how we communicate, and how we express our love. When we don't know or honor ourselves, we rely on others to see us for who they want us to be. That's dangerous, because we often adhere to their version of us while letting ourselves down. Going down that path is never worth it.

Defining authenticity is simple, but the daily practice of living it out isn't. It requires us to answer the question, "Who am I?" This question challenges us to move past the titles we've acquired in life and think about the people who have shaped us, the experiences that changed us, our talents and weaknesses, and our values. The beautiful but emotionally exhausting thing about this is that as life evolves, so does our understanding of ourselves. This is why authenticity is a lifelong process of coming home to ourselves.

One main consequence of being authentic and vulnerable is that some people won't like the authentic version of you—and you must become okay with it. Will there be people who don't hire you, don't want to listen to your message, or discount you because of your authentic self? Probably! But you must refuse to carry that story into the spaces you go, because you will automatically put yourself at a disadvantage. **Refuse to own other people's insecurity.** Trust that your authenticity will open and close all the right doors for you.

If authenticity is a deep knowing of who you are, then vulnerability is having the courage to let people see that version of you. Vulnerability is the door you walk through to stand center stage in your life. It's the invitation you give people to join you and experience what you're thinking, feeling, and believing.

Too many people keep that door shut out of fear of what other people will think of them. This is why people stay silent, and silence is one of the biggest threats to building trust. How so? Because our silence leaves people second-guessing. Vulnerability is the permission we give ourselves not to leave people second-guessing. It's the opinion we share in a meeting. It's the feelings you share with your partner. It is the thought you stand up and share in front of a group because you trust that someone in that room needs to hear your message in only the way you can say it. And it's the truth you tell yourself about what you need for your emotional well-being.

Vulnerability isn't always comfortable. Frankly, being vulnerable might bring about tears, heartburn, or bubble guts (okay, my mom is going to get on me for using that word). But it'll also make you feel lighter, and you'll respect yourself a little more every time you show your vulnerability. The relationships worth your time and attention should always want you to show up authentically.

Authenticity and vulnerability are the antidotes to every person who has ever felt invisible. People see you differently when you learn to see yourself!

3. Live what you love.

This isn't fluff or a feel-good mantra. It's a foundational strategy for any manager who builds trust seeking to build authentic relationships between themselves and their team. It's about consciously making choices that align with your values and passions rather than conforming to external expectations and getting so busy being busy that you lose yourself in the process.

There will be moments on your journey when you come face-to-face with your integrity, and your values will be tested. This is where you find out what you really stand for. These moments won't be easy, but they'll teach you a lot about yourself.

When you're clear about your core four values, you'll navigate challenges with greater conviction and inspire stronger confidence from your team. Living in congruence with one's values builds trust and will always foster respect.

Are you ready for this next one? Okay, I'm going to need you to get a hobby! I don't care if it's reading, bird watching, photography, gardening, woodworking, or working out. Just find something that fires you up! Without it, you're likely to burn out. Hobbies and passions aren't just "nice to have" pastimes; they're your lifeline to thinking clearly and staying grounded. Look up any research on the power of hobbies, and you'll see clear evidence for how hobbies help us generate more innovative insights and ideas, promote stress relief, and help us feel better.

You're more than just your work. If you don't have a hobby, find something that interests you. If you do have one, make time for it. Not only will you benefit, you'll also be a role model to your team, demonstrating that life outside of work is also important.

4. Recharge your energy.

Part of you showing up your best is knowing when you're no longer in the flow. In the moments where you're struggling to concentrate, you don't feel present, or you're feeling fatigued, you need to take a break. Your body is telling you what it needs, and it's up to you to listen.

Taking breaks doesn't make you a slacker; it makes you efficient. Anyone who thinks differently has yet to look at the science. Current research on "ultradian rhythm" recommends a ninety-minute productivity block followed by twenty minutes of rest and renewal. If you can't make twenty minutes, then go for five to ten minutes. Any break is better than nothing.

Note, though, that scrolling through social media isn't a break. You need actions that allow you to decompress and chill cognitively. You can do small tasks, but it shouldn't require much cognitive effort. Some easy decompression ideas are to:

- Go for a walk.
- Doodle, color, or draw.
- Take a shower or bath.
- Listen to feel-good music .
- Meditate.
- Take a power nap.
- Make a gratitude list.
- Recognize someone for their efforts.

Be mindful of how you schedule and agree to meetings on your calendar. If you're in back-to-back meetings all day, you need to set stronger boundaries with yourself. Does every meeting need to be an hour? What if you only schedule thirty-minute meetings, or wrap up an hour-long meeting at the fifty-minute mark?

We've all experienced the consequences of ignoring our energy levels and grinding through. We often become irritable, lack creativity, and experience our overall satisfaction levels slowly decreasing. Everyone loses. Managers who build trust pay attention to their energy levels and recharge when necessary.

5. Set boundaries when necessary.

I'd like to invite you to rethink the very idea of "boundaries." Boundaries aren't about you being a jerk or pushing your own agenda. Boundaries are about you loving yourself and other people enough to be transparent about what's okay and what's not okay. Boundaries are like traffic signs. They tell us and others when to slow down, when we need to stop, and what's off-limits. Boundaries are not just nice guidelines; they're nonnegotiables for keeping the peace.

If you don't set and enforce your boundaries, you're telling yourself that everyone else's time, needs, and priorities are more important than yours. That's not humility; that's self-sabotage. Setting solid boundaries is the ultimate self-respect move. It means valuing your time and energy enough to guard them fiercely. When you do that, something amazing happens. You start to attract people who respect your boundaries because they see you respecting yourself. When you feel disrespected, stressed, or overwhelmed, I want you to stop and ask yourself, "What boundary can I create that would better serve me?"

I once had a coaching client who was addicted to his work. He would come home and still be responding to emails, distracted from the people he loved the most. He decided to set a boundary for himself to be more present. He called it his "No Fly Zone." He chose a two-hour window when he was home where he didn't engage with any technology at all. After a short time, he realized his work never suffered. If anything, his team members were thankful he'd stopped sending stuff to them after work hours! His relationship with his family improved, and he was happier with life overall.

I have someone I adore on my team who at first didn't take initiative as quickly as I wanted, often seeking explicit permission before moving forward on anything. We had a productive conversation, and I realized a lot of that behavior came from her being micromanaged before joining my team. I'm not that manager, and I needed her to show up differently if our professional relationship would continue. I empathized and then set a boundary with her that unless it had to do with money, she had my permission to run with things, and I would support her. That boundary left her feeling empowered, clarified what we both needed from each other, and improved the relationship.

Maybe some of you need to set a boundary around self-care, how you allow people to communicate with you, or how you manage your work calendar. A manager who builds trust knows that the key to building authentic relationships with others is building an authentic relationship with themselves. Setting boundaries is one way they consistently show up for themselves.

BUILDING THE RELATIONSHIP WITH YOUR TEAM

The success of your relationships with your team will largely dictate the success of your leadership. It's much easier to help people become more self-aware and take accountability when they believe you care for them and have their back in the process. **When your team trusts your intentions, they will follow you, not out of obligation but out of belief.** That makes a big difference!

One of the best managers I ever had was named Aaron. He expected us to deliver great results and pay attention to details. That man would know if my spacing in a PowerPoint presentation was a centimeter off, and he would catch it every darn time! But, he made me a better performer. Aaron taught me a masterclass on how **the best managers push you while also making you feel cared for in the process.** I never questioned his care for me and others on the team. He always made time for us. He ensured we had the tools and knowledge to be successful. He created opportunities for people on the team to build relationships with each other.

Every great manager I've ever worked with has always kept sight of their humanity, regardless of what was happening inside the organization. Their humanity was their most differentiating gift. When we lose our humanity, we lose our ability to connect. It can feel natural to shut off our hearts and only lead from our heads when trying to protect ourselves and the company. But there's a cost associated with that behavior.

Recently, we've seen in the news the dangerous impact of leaders forgetting their humanity. We've seen three college presidents focus more on legalese than just saying what they really believed about hate speech, and what was the humane thing to do on their campuses. As a result, they were condemned, and two resigned. We've witnessed Google lay off around six percent of its workforce by simply invalidating their login passwords versus having an honest conversation with them first. The founder and CEO of Kyte Baby fired an employee who asked to work remotely because her baby was in the neonatal intensive care unit. The CEO came out with a scripted statement that caused even more backlash. She then finally dropped the script and remembered her humanity. She issued another statement where she said, "I was insensitive, selfish, and only focused on the fact that her job had always been done on-site, and I did not see the possibility of doing it remotely."

We want our employees to be loyal and engaged, but then we don't show up for them. Our team members are not cogs in a gear to be used solely for our benefit. We'll never build authentic relationships that way. Employees give us their time, energy, and commitment, and they expect their leaders to reciprocate.

Greg Creed, former CEO of Yum! Brands, said, "The customer's experience will never exceed the team member's experience." Don't expect your team to deliver a five-star experience when they're not getting one. Energy attracts like energy. Greg taught me that managers who build trust view their team members as their primary customers. They do everything they can to ensure their team has a great experience. When that happens, those team members will turn around and provide a similar experience to the company's customers.

Make Consistent Trust Deposits

If you want to build meaningful relationships with the people on your team, you must intentionally make consistent trust deposits into those relationships. You must be intentional every day at building authentic relationships with your employees, both as individuals and as part of a team. When you create these relationships, you learn to see each other as real people (both inside and outside work), and the connection is mutually beneficial.

Great managers understand that they must earn the right to lead people, regardless of title and position. Their primary focus is on building meaningful relationships rooted in trust. Creating this trust allows managers to uncover issues, push team members harder, provide and receive relevant feedback, engage in hard conversations when necessary, and develop the kind of influence that leads to more productive performance.

We live in a world where it's too easy to focus on the work over the person. But the more you focus on the person, the better the work becomes. Building authentic relationships starts during the interview process, is confirmed in your onboarding process, and continues throughout the relationship's life cycle.

In Stephen Covey's book, *The 7 Habits of Highly Effective People*, he talks about the concept of "emotional bank accounts." He calls it "a metaphor that describes the amount of trust that's been built up in a relationship. It's the feeling of safeness you have with another human being." Managers must intentionally make consistent deposits into these relationship bank accounts with the people who report to them. These trust deposits lead to increased engagement, honest conversations, and an environment people never want to leave. Without these deposits, managers often experience higher turnover, and their people perform because of compliance instead of commitment. Many of us have worked for a manager who didn't make trust deposits. It's miserable!

Managers must consistently make trust deposits because, on certain days, they'll need to make withdrawals. In those cases, you want to ensure there are enough deposits in the account to prevent an overdraft. All relationships end when people become emotionally bankrupt, whether in personal life or at a company. In those situations, people will risk starting a brand-new relationship simply in the hopes that that new person is willing to make those trust deposits. Building authentic relationships and keeping them requires you to invest in the relationship consistently.

Below are ten actions you can immediately take to make intentional trust deposits.

1. Send a note/text/email or call to let them know you appreciate them.
2. Celebrate personal and professional milestones/successes.
3. Be fully present when talking (point your feet directly at them).
4. Stay curious and ask follow-up questions.
5. Ask them what they're doing to prioritize self-care.
6. Ask them for their opinions and ideas.
7. Apologize when you need to take accountability for something.
8. Surprise them with a small, thoughtful gift that aligns with their interests.
9. Invite them to lunch so you can get to know them better.
10. Show interest in their life outside of work.

Additionally, below are actual examples of what I've seen other leaders do to build relationships with their teams. I hope some of the examples will inspire you to do something similar.

Onboarding Process

You can build trust from the interview process to how someone is onboarded inside your organization. These deposits show them the type of leader you are and what your culture is all about. I remember signing the offer letter to join Yum! Brands in 2012. Shortly afterward, and before I ever started my first day on the job, I received a colorful bouquet of cookies (designed as pizzas, chickens, and tacos) at my house with a letter from my manager that read, "Welcome to the Yum family." It made me feel valued, and her action instantly reaffirmed that I had made the right decision to join the company. She remodeled for me that building relationships starts from the moment someone is hired and before they formally begin their first day.

Letters to Parents

Former PepsiCo CEO Indra Nooyi wrote personal letters to the parents of her senior executives. She knew that most high performers and executives never received this type of recognition, and she believed they deserved it. She acknowledged that parents have a lot to do with their children's success, so she wanted them to know how much she appreciated their contributions. She thanked them for the gift of their child at PepsiCo. Those personal letters were a genuine hit. The parents felt proud. Her staff felt appreciated. It was a win-win for everyone.

A Family Invitation

I met a Taco Bell restaurant manager who would invite the immediate family of every new hire to have either lunch/ dinner with him. He wanted the employees to understand that they were joining a restaurant family and that this was a place where you could bring your whole self to work. Therefore, he wanted to get to know them and their family.

Virtual Team Lunches

During the COVID-19 pandemic, many people worked from home, and managers were trying to learn how to lead effectively in a virtual environment. My best friend's company decided to do virtual lunches once a month. The CEO would send everyone a gift card to order their lunch through one of the food apps and have it delivered to their home. During the virtual lunch, there was no talk about work. It was a time to build community and connect. The employees played games, recognized people in the company, had trivia if a holiday or significant event was coming up, highlighted any new hires that had joined that month, and the CEO would address any pivotal current events going on at the time and remind people he was there to talk with them if they needed to talk.

Compassion During Tragedy

Nothing in leadership training prepares you for what to do when a team member dies or loses someone they love. I remember when a colleague of mine unexpectedly lost her mother. Her direct supervisor was there for her every step of the way. She did all the expected things like talking with her, sending flowers and a card, and asking how she could best support her during that moment. But she went even further. My friend had planned to take a vacation later in the year but ended up using more time off to deal with her mother's passing than she expected. She went to her boss after the funeral and bereavement period and told her she wasn't going to go on her vacation since she used all of her time. Her manager immediately showed compassion and said, "Absolutely not. You need to take that time and enjoy it with your family." My friend talked about her manager's compassion many times to other people. That one trust deposit into the relationship cemented her loyalty and respect for her manager.

Virtual Team-Building Activities

Jēnna Reese is the founder and CEO of Connect Centric. She has implemented some of the most creative virtual team-building activities I've witnessed from a manager. She hired a chocolatier from Dallmann Fine Chocolates for her team holiday party one year. That individual delivered a box of chocolate to each person's home address. Everyone hopped on a virtual video call, and the chocolatier walked the entire team through each type of chocolate, made them describe the smells and taste, and explained how each was made. The team laughed throughout, asked questions, and people were sharing their experiences. It led to a great session where the team got to know each other outside of just their work.

Jēnna also used the company Confetti to plan her winter holiday party. It's a website where you can choose different virtual experiences for your team. She chose the "Winter holidays around the world." She said they all jumped on a virtual call, and the person guiding the activities took them through all different types of holidays worldwide, engaged in polls and trivia, and made the session interactive. It was an organic way to build connections and more diverse thinking on the team.

BUILDING THE RELATIONSHIP WITH OTHERS ACROSS THE ORGANIZATION

Building relationships across the organization isn't about "playing nice" or schmoozing. It's about forging alliances and creating a web of support that helps stuff get done and is mutually beneficial for everyone involved. For managers who build trust, it's strategic. It means you've got your finger on the pulse of the company, understanding the undercurrents, and the "stuff" that never makes it to a memo. These relationships are your intel; they tell you who's got the skills for the job, who's up for a challenge, and where the hidden obstacles lie.

Managers who build trust don't wait for influence to happen. They make the first move. They understand that strategic moves lead to movements, and that this is how you change people and spaces for the better.

Below are four actions to build relationships across the organization and create the influence you want.

1. Build trust.

If you've read my book, *Your Road to Yes!: How to Build Trust in Yourself and with Others*, then you know trust is built in the small, everyday moments of how we show up and treat each other. More specifically, trust is built when you communicate with three important Ts:

1. Transparency
2. Tact
3. Togetherness

We don't have the luxury of focusing on just one of these factors. High levels of trust in our relationships require all three.

Communicating with transparency requires you to share your point of view and explain the why behind it. Trust never leaves people second-guessing. When you feel others are holding back or not sharing, you can ask a question to prompt their transparency. I might ask, "What do you think? I'd love to get your thoughts on this." Or "What am I missing or not thinking about?" These techniques are simple ways to take people along the journey with you.

Communicating with tact requires you to make people feel safe. Your presence is either going to put people at ease or put them on edge. Those are your only two options. I'm constantly reminding myself to remove the judgment from my tone and create space in the conversation because gentleness will take me much further than fear ever will.

Communicating with togetherness is how you make people feel we're all in the same boat, rowing in the same direction. It's your ability to make people feel like they're part of a team. And shouldn't that always be the goal? A few actions demonstrating this include showing empathy, recognizing them for their contributions, caring enough to engage in hard conversations if necessary, and making yourself available and reminding them they're not alone. From my experience, once togetherness starts to break down in a relationship, so does both transparency and tact.

2. Deliver Value.

Zappos built a wildly successful customer service model by consistently delivering WOW to their customers. Their model was built on three pillars:

1. Be accurate.
2. Be easy.
3. Be personal.

Managers who build trust deliver repeated value. If you want to build authentic relationships across the organization, you must show up and deliver value.

Being accurate looks like being knowledgeable in your area, consistently delivering what you promise, communicating transparently so everyone knows what to expect, and having a point of view that moves the conversation forward.

Being easy to work with means you manage your intensity when it starts to get the best of you, you're timely in your responses to people, you have a "one point of contact" mindset so you're not sending people to others to get things resolved, and you listen deeply when people speak.

Being personal happens when you demonstrate empathy, recognize others for their effort, reach out to connect, and care about them just as much personally as you do professionally.

My company, The Trust Architect Group, adopted this business model. We rate ourselves (on a scale of 1 to 5) at the end of every year on how we feel we did in each of the three areas. We then make strategic decisions on moving those scores up for the following year so that we continue to deliver exceptional value to each other and to our clients.

3. Communicate Well.

My pastor once said, "You can't meet people where they are when you think you're above them." That stuck! Great communication and relationship-building never ask you to give up who you are, but you do have to flex your style and be willing to meet people where they are. Doing so often opens the door for deeper, more compassionate listening and understanding.

I'm biased since I teach D.I.S.C. communication workshops, but I think every manager benefits by knowing the four communication styles. It helps leaders understand how to meet people where they are. You don't have to go through the workshop to be a better communicator. Since humans are different but very predictable, you simply need to be able to answer two fundamental questions:

1. Is the person task- or people-focused?
2. Is the person slower- or faster-paced?

You can quickly determine if the person you're talking to is trying to get right down to business, or if they want to spend a few minutes connecting first. Meet them where they are. You can also pick up on their cues when they are going slower and need space in the conversation to think. Or when they're fast-paced and just want a high-level overview of things. Meet them where they are.

4. Create Visibility.

People can't celebrate or rally around things they don't know. Please don't wait for others to help you be seen. It's up to you to create a window into your and your team's work so people can see it. It's not braggadocios. It's effective leadership.

Here are a few ways managers who build trust create visibility:

Introduction Gush

There will be moments when you find yourself in a group setting where people don't know each other. It could be at a conference, a networking event, or a business meeting. If you're with someone you know well, you have an opportunity to create visibility for that person and make them look like a star in front of others. It might not open a door for them, but it sure does create a window that allows them to see that person differently. Those window moments matter!

You don't need to say everything you know about the person. You're trying to say enough to intrigue the person to ask more or open a conversation. After all, it's called an "Introduction Gush" for a reason. You must have a level of enthusiasm and passion for the person you're talking about. Use the following three-step formula as a guide, but feel free to make it your own so your words feel natural.

1. This is my friend (say name with excitement).
2. She/He is (articulate one professional achievement that lends to credibility).
3. And she/he (name one personal note that is unique about the person).

Examples of an Introduction Gush:

- "Have you met my friend, Jenna? Her company is changing how organizations implement technology to create better customer experiences. She's also your go-to person if you ever want to travel to Italy, since she's been so many times."
- "I want to introduce you to Ross. He's so humble that he'll never tell you he's written over fifty books and is one

of only a handful of professional speakers that has spoken on every continent. He also has fascinating stories of professional athletes he's met and worked with over the years."

- "Hi, Jane. I want to introduce you to my team member, Jeff. He's the mastermind behind the new operational process you were just talking about that we recently rolled out. He's also one of the most creative, out-of-the-box thinkers I know."

Success Spotlights

Creating visibility into the work your team is doing isn't just about giving credit; it's a strategic move that positions you as a leader who is not only proud but intentional. It's about crafting a narrative of success that resonates throughout the organization, showcasing the commitment, creativity, and collective effort that defines your team. It's about genuinely acknowledging the hard work and success that might otherwise go unnoticed.

You have a chance every week to highlight the success and milestones of others. By genuinely recognizing others, you're also shining a spotlight on the type of leader you are and the work being produced. Think of your spotlights as a billboard that others get to drive by and quickly see. It's just one glimpse into your world, but it's repeated glimpses over time that help you build your brand and relationships.

A few simple ways you can spotlight success include:

- Use social media to highlight people on your team, peers, or even your customers.
- Send an email up the organization, spotlighting the work someone on your team did.

- Write a monthly newsletter where you highlight what and who you're proud of in a section.
- Spend a few minutes in your team meetings creating space for people to recognize each other.

Monthly Recaps

One common theme between every manager I've coached is that none of them ever wanted to feel blindsided. They didn't feel the need to be in all the details, but they wanted to be in the loop on what was happening. Your manager will feel the same.

Managers who build trust know visibility is something you create, not something you wait for. So in those one-on-ones with their boss, they find organic ways to highlight the sweat equity the team is putting in.

Make a habit of sharing two wins, two watch-outs, and one recognition with your manager. Highlight two wins since your last meeting and two watch-outs you want to loop your manager in on and discuss if needed, then end with recognizing someone on your team or in the organization. This model allows you to be brief and brilliant while fostering a proactive culture of communication and appreciation.

Creating visibility isn't about patting yourself on the back; it's about ensuring the work your team is producing doesn't fade into the background. It's about ensuring the higher-ups see the time, effort, and results the way you do.

Contribute to the Conversation

Managers who build trust understand that visibility is not just about being seen; it's about being heard. By seizing speaking opportunities, they amplify their voice and the voice of their team. They understand that this exposure often begets more opportunities, and that's good for them and their team because they can share some of that spotlight and opportunity with others.

Writing blogs and articles allows you the chance to highlight your point of view on your area of expertise, spark dialogue, and expand your thinking in the process.

Use social media, especially professional networks like LinkedIn, to your advantage. They serve as a digital stage for you to share your thought leadership. It's where ideas are not just presented but interacted with, and where a manager's profile becomes a testament to their expertise. Does your digital presence showcase the trajectory of your knowledge and experience? Every click, like, share, and comment is an opportunity to build your brand. Make it count.

Managers who build trust aren't idle bystanders waiting for connections to form organically. They are the architects of their relationships. They are intentional about consistently showing up and building relationships with their team and others across the organization. They don't see "building relationships" as just another bullet point on a long to-do list. They understand that their role extends far beyond mere task delegation or project management. By taking the lead, reaching out, and connecting with individuals at all levels, they lay the groundwork for their team's success and contribute to a culture of trust and belonging. And that's how they bring out the best in people and their performance.

CHAPTER SUMMARY

- Management is all about people and performance. You can value excellence and results while still putting people first.
- Building meaningful relationships is going to require you to master the art of consistently showing up for yourself and others.
- You can't be a manager who builds trust and emotionally disconnected at the same time.
- Five actions to building the relationship with yourself include:
  1. Honor who you are at your best.
  2. Develop authentic confidence.
  3. Live what you love.
  4. Recharge your energy.
  5. Set boundaries when necessary.
- If you want to build meaningful relationships with the people on your team, you must be intentional about making consistent trust deposits into those relationships.
- The best managers push you while also making you feel cared for in the process.
- Building authentic relationships starts during the interview process, is confirmed in your onboarding process, and continues throughout the relationship's life cycle.
- Managers who build trust don't wait for influence to just happen. They make the first move.
- Four ways managers build relationships across the organization include:
  1. Build trust
  2. Deliver value
  3. Communicate well
  4. Create visibility

FIVE

Be clear with people
On what you expect and need.
They can handle it.

PLAY 2:
SET CLEAR EXPECTATIONS

I once worked for a manager who was great at building relationships but could've done a better job setting clear expectations. The result was collective frustration among the team. She was managing the best she knew how, but she was moving so quickly that she never thought through what she wanted or expected as a final outcome. As a result, people would leave her office and take action based on vague expectations. When they met again, she would keep revising her expectations because she was gaining more clarity herself. It caused endless revisions and a lack of productivity.

That experience taught me that building authentic relationships is vital, but so is setting clear boundaries and goals. When managers fail at this, they set everyone up for failure, including themselves. Managers who build trust slow down and take the necessary time to clarify what they're asking people to do and why. **Excellent performance is a result of clear expectations.**

Brené Brown defines boundaries as communicating what's okay and what isn't, and states that "boundary-setting is a practice." That's precisely what we're doing when we communicate expectations with each other. Setting clear boundaries is not a one-time event where you establish your needs and never discuss them again. It's an ongoing practice of checking in, recognizing others when they do things well, encouraging others to ask clarifying questions, and leaning into uncomfortable conversations when we need to realign.

I find that most employees rise to the level of expectations managers have of them. A few come up short, and the superstars will always over-deliver. But it's ultimately your job as a manager who builds trust to set these expectations.

Managers who build trust don't see setting clear expectations as a "do this or else" objective. It's a collaborative effort to understand what we need from each other, so that everyone's set up for success.

The Most Common Mistake When Setting Expectations

The most common mistake when setting expectations is not being clear enough. Vague goals or instructions can lead to confusion and inconsistency in performance. It's often the silent underminer of potential for both an individual and an entire team.

Let's look at some examples of vague expectations by managers:

- "Just get it done to the best of your ability."
- "I need you to be a team player."
- "Please be punctual to all meetings."
- "Get that to me by the end of the week."
- "Try to be a positive influence on the team."

These expectations are too vague and don't provide specific details about what they are being asked to do, or how they will be evaluated. As a result, team members may not understand what's really expected of them, and struggle to meet the ideals you have in your head. As a result, you'll both grow increasingly frustrated with the work and with each other. Setting clear expectations is not about establishing a rigid framework. It's about fostering a culture where clarity is valued, and everyone contributes to helping shape the path forward.

Two Main Types of Managerial Expectations

There are two types of expectations every manager needs to set:

- Performance expectations *(what you do)*
- Behavioral expectations *(how you do it)*

Performance expectations identify *what* you should focus on to achieve success. Great managers clearly communicate a vision of the end result, not the detailed process for how someone achieves that end result. The best managers allow space for team members to bring their unique skills, creativity, and ideas for completing tasks successfully. Managers should only dictate the process when associates must follow specific safety, consistency, or measurability steps.

Below are three examples of thorough performance expectations by managers for employees:

1. "Before you interact with clients, you'll need to complete all online onboarding training in the four-week timeframe outlined. You must pass the knowledge test with a minimum score of ninety percent."

2. "I want you and Amir to collaborate on a team development strategy for the rest of the year. The goal is to help our staff communicate in a way that builds more trust. I'm open to any format. We don't have a budget for additional development, so I want to use our current people and resources. Can you put together an initial plan and present it to me in two weeks?"

3. "I'm a coaching leader who relies on candor. I believe people grow through honest, heart-centered feedback. You can expect a weekly one-on-one with me, and I'll provide feedback when appropriate. You can also expect I'll ask for feedback on my own performance."

Behavioral expectations identify *how* you should show up in the process of driving results. These expectations signal the behavior and actions that are okay and not okay. I've coached many "high performers" who were excellent at meeting performance expectations but not nearly as mindful of the behaviors they demonstrated to get those results. To be honest, I used to be one of those individuals.

Organizations should hold all employees responsible for both *what* and *how* they achieve. In my organization, we commit to our clients that we'll be accurate, easy to work with, and personable. Those are the behavioral expectations we've established for ourselves, and we measure our success against those expectations at the end of each year. We also agree to give each other feedback when we've veered away from those behavioral expectations. All managers should establish behavioral expectations for at least the following three topics:

- How you interact with other colleagues
- How you conduct yourself on social media
- Your professional image/hygiene

Meeting Expectations

Managers must set clear expectations and ensure their teams have enough resources and knowledge to meet those expectations. You set up team members and the entire business for failure if there's a gap between those two topics.

Start asking your team members if they have the resources and knowledge to complete what you've asked them to. Encourage employees to ask clarifying questions about your expectations, such as:

- "What is the allotted budget for this?"
- "What is the expected timeline?"
- "How will we measure success?"
- "How does this align with our current or future strategy?"

Your expectations might need to change as the business changes. Give yourself permission to reimagine and readdress expectations as needed. Make it safe for your team to come to you and tell you they're not meeting expectations, or they need something different to do so at the level you want.

Remember earlier when I told you that you're a trust architect? Well, trust architects lay out a clear path to success and don't leave people second-guessing. Being specific, consistent, and realistic in your expectations can create a deeper sense of accountability and trust within your team. When that happens, performance improves, and everyone wins.

CHAPTER SUMMARY

- Excellent performance is a result of clear expectations.
- Setting clear expectations is not a one-time event. It's an ongoing practice of checking in.
- Managers who build trust see setting clear expectations as a collaborative effort to understand what we need from each other so that everyone is set up for success.
- The most common mistake when setting expectations is not being clear enough. Vague goals or instructions can lead to confusion and inconsistency in performance.
- There are two types of expectations every manager needs to set: performance and behavioral.
- Performance expectations identify *what* you should focus on to achieve success.
- Behavioral expectations identify *how* you should show up in the process of driving results.
- Managers must set clear expectations, but they must also ensure their teams have enough resources and knowledge to meet those expectations.
- Your expectations might need to change as the business changes. Give yourself permission to reimagine and readdress expectations as needed.

SIX

Love people enough
To tell them your truth on how
They are showing up.

PLAY 3:
LEAN INTO PERFORMANCE CONVERSATIONS

Managers who build trust must have the discernment to know which type of performance conversations they need to engage in with each employee in order to drive stronger performance and accountability. We spend so much time building authentic relationships to earn trust and create a safe environment to have these types of meaningful conversations.

Effective communication always creates space for deeper levels of awareness and empowers forward movement. There are several types of conversations all managers who build trust must lean into consistently:

- Feedback conversations
- Coaching conversations
- Teaching and mentoring conversations
- Difficult conversations

FEEDBACK CONVERSATIONS

The most common type of performance conversation you'll engage in as a manager is a feedback conversation. All employees need both positive and constructive feedback if they are to grow to their full potential. You will engage in feedback conversations during one-on-ones, performance reviews, difficult conversations, and informal situations where you're having lunch, walking around the office, or writing a thank-you note.

Feedback is nothing more than me sharing information with you about what you're doing well or what you need to do differently so you can improve. A boss once told me, "All feedback is just information. You get to decide what you do with it."

Feedback plays a critical role in both management and employee success. You owe it to your employees and the company to provide positive and constructive feedback. However, please only offer one type of feedback at a time. If you provide positive feedback, let it be that and celebrate one's achievement. If you provide constructive feedback, don't muddy your message with additional talking points. The goal is for the associate to hear what you're saying. I'm not a proponent of the "sandwich technique," where you start by telling them something good, tell them what they need to improve on, and then end with another positive. Most people have enough awareness to know what you're doing, so this technique feels disingenuous. There are also associates who will only hear and take away the positive feedback, and they miss the meat of what you were trying to communicate.

Managers rely on the sandwich technique when they're unsure how to deliver feedback, assuming that this approach will make it more comfortable. But here's the hard truth: **managing effectively isn't about being comfortable.** When you're worried about making yourself or others feel comfortable, you often don't tell the truth and engage in the conversations you need to have. As a manager, being liked isn't always possible in every moment. You owe it to yourself, the other person, and the organization to be uncomfortable when necessary.

In 2023, I heard Anne Davis Gotte, Vice President of Human Resources at General Mills, beautifully articulate why managers need to focus on being kind but not confuse that with being nice:

> "We sometimes use the terms 'kind' and 'nice' synonymous. And in doing so, we've gotten it wrong. Nice is safe. Nice is afraid. Nice is about fitting in at any cost. Kind is brave. Kind is clear. Kind is honest. Kind cares enough to be uncomfortable and give you critical feedback. When we're worried about being nice, we really screw up because all we do is try to 'smooth over' the cracks, but the cracks are still there. Kindness is about caring enough to land a message that's deeply uncomfortable and doing it with as much empathy as you can so that it lands as well as it can for them. Kind might sound like, 'I'm so uncomfortable and worried about how to say this because I'm afraid I might hurt your feelings, but I care enough to try it anyway.'"

Feedback is crucial for everyone's growth, and being a manager who builds trust requires us to give feedback to others. **Delivering useful feedback requires three primary factors:**

1. Creating an environment of safety
2. Addressing the specific behavior
3. Highlighting the impact of that behavior

In their "20-Minute Manager" series chapter titled "Giving Effective Feedback," the editors of *The Harvard Business Review* said, "Feedback is most likely to have a positive, lasting effect when its focus is on behavior that the recipient is able to change and its delivery is well timed."

Feedback conversations can happen informally and formally. However, I recommend you find ways to bring feedback into the conversations you're already having organically. Here are three examples of how you might do so.

Feedback Example 1: You're in a one-on-one meeting, discussing a project someone's working on. You might say, "Hey, about that project. I've been wanting to tell you, I noticed how you slowed down in the last meeting to make sure everyone had their questions answered. That seemed to be a good way to let you gain buy-in moving forward. I'm proud of you for that, and other leadership team members noticed too."

Feedback Example 2: A team member admits they're struggling on a project. They've opened the door for you. You might start by saying, "I'm glad you brought that up. It says a lot about your level of self-awareness, which you know I respect. I've noticed that in our one-on-ones, you consistently say you have the time, resources, and knowledge to meet the upcoming deadlines, but then they're missed. I find myself confused and admittedly sometimes frustrated about why this is happening. I need to be clear that the business can no longer afford to delay this project. Help me understand what's going on, and how I can help you get this project back on track."

Feedback Example 3: If there's no natural way to weave the feedback into your conversation, then address it head-on by saying, "I committed to you when we first started working together that I'd always be honest with you and help you grow in the organization. In that spirit, I've noticed that the last several emails you've sent out to the client were overly direct, and the tone came across as angry. I believe this will impact your relationship with the client if this continues, and it will also impact how they view our organization. One of our core values is communicating with both head and heart, but it feels like the heart piece is sometimes missing in your communications. Can you tell me more about what's going on?"

You'll notice that at the end of the constructive feedback, I ask a question or ask for their help in understanding why something is happening. The primary reason is that I'm placing the responsibility in the lap of the person I'm talking with. The secondary reason is that I want them to know we're in this together.

Make feedback a regular part of your management style. Teach your team what effective feedback sounds like. Ask your employees for feedback on your approach. Provide them with feedback that's positive far more often than constructive. If you do this, they'll trust your intent when you come to them with a more difficult conversation.

COACHING CONVERSATIONS

Great managers are great coaches. Coaching is fundamentally how we build self-efficacy and confidence in team members. Most leaders I've worked with think they're coaching when they give feedback and share opinions. While there's a time and place for that, coaching conversations are entirely different.

Managers should engage in coaching conversations with employees when they don't know how to get from Point A to Point B. You'll know someone needs coaching when you can identify the gap between where they are today and where they want to be in the future. Examples include:

- They don't understand the next step to take on a project.
- They're struggling in a relationship with someone at work.
- They're confused about the right next step in their career.
- They want to be more assertive but don't know what actions to take.

The goal in these examples is to move the person from where they feel stuck to where they can take decisive action.

Coaching is not about giving people the answers or trying to "fix" them. People don't need to be fixed. They need to be heard and allowed to self-discover their next right answer. You already know that people are more likely to take decisive action and follow through on commitments when they're the ones who created them. This is how we build a culture of accountability. As a manager, you can aid that process by listening deeply, asking open-ended questions that get the individual to look at themselves and the situation in a safe way, acknowledging their feelings and perspectives, and asking them what they feel the next right step is to get where they say they want to be.

The types of questions you ask during a coaching conversation matter. We want to focus on asking open-ended questions, ones that start with "who," "what," "when," "where," "why," or "how." However, although "how" and "why" questions are open-ended, they also require the person to spend a lot of time rehashing the past, which isn't always necessary in managerial coaching. **The goal of coaching should be to get people thinking differently about the topic now, then understanding what needs to happen in the future.** Marion Franklin, author of the wonderful book *The Heart of Laser-Focused Coaching*, discusses how every question we ask should challenge the person we're coaching to think more deeply and to explore the topic in a way they previously have not. To do that, Franklin recommends starting your questions with the word "what," explaining, "A what question becomes incredibly powerful when it forces the client to think about something in a new way, rather than tell you something they already know." Take the following questions, for example:

- What did you want to gain when you made that choice?
- What do you know now that you didn't know previously?
- What does that person need to hear from you that maybe they haven't heard?
- What do you need to forgive yourself for so you can move forward?
- What choice would you make if you felt confident and powerful?

These sample questions create the space for the person you're coaching to think about the topic in a deeper, more meaningful way. You don't need a list of questions to ask. You only need to show up, be present, and stay curious. When you're curious, you can piggyback right off what the person just said and ask a powerful open-ended question. Most managers I know don't ask enough questions, and when they do, they're usually trying to lead the other person into doing what they believe they should do. That's not coaching; that's manipulation. Managers who build trust hold space for others and ask thoughtful, forward-thinking questions. Spend time over the next month listening to the types of questions you ask. When in doubt, start your question with the word "what."

TEACHING AND MENTORING CONVERSATIONS

Two other types of performance conversations you'll need to have with your employees regularly are teaching and mentoring. Both conversations require you to take your current knowledge and impart it to others. This fundamentally differs from coaching because in that case, you're not giving people the answers. In teaching and mentoring conversations, you explicitly are sharing what's worked for you based on past experiences.

Teaching and mentoring conversations are just as meaningful as other types for an associate's growth and development. Managers should engage in teaching conversations when a team member is unaware of company processes or history, and when the only way for them to learn it is if someone sits down and directly teaches it to them. Additionally, a teaching conversation is relevant if an associate needs more knowledge to perform a role effectively.

Sometimes, a manager might not be the best person to teach the associate, so they have a responsibility to find the people who are. Managers should engage in mentoring conversations when they feel sharing their experience with a team member might close a knowledge gap and possibly provide a new way of doing things. The goal of mentoring conversations is not to make your associates like you, but to offer fresh perspectives, encourage action, expose them to more people and opportunities, helping to unleash the potential already inside them.

DIFFICULT CONVERSATIONS

You'll know it's time to have a difficult conversation when the issue at hand is significantly affecting the team or an individual's performance, when it's clear that the problem won't resolve itself without intervention, and when the potential negative impact of not addressing the issue outweighs the discomfort of the conversation. It's also the right time if you've observed a pattern of behavior detrimental to the work environment, if all other means of feedback have led to failure, or if the situation has a sense of urgency and that delaying the conversation could lead to further complications.

Difficult conversations are often associated with higher emotional stakes than any other type of performance conversation, which means we might have to address confrontation, deeply held beliefs, or significant personal or professional impacts. Due to this, many managers shy away from having difficult conversations. Stewing in silence won't serve you or your relationships. You owe it to the other person and the business to have difficult conversations when necessary.

Difficult conversations will be a part of your entire leadership journey. They never go away. The higher you climb in the organization, the more often you'll be engaged in them. So many people want to learn how to engage in these conversations and be comfortable, but I don't think it's about being comfortable. These are hard talks because you care about the outcome, you care about the relationship, and you're not sure how the other person will take it, which makes them inherently uncomfortable. **Difficult conversations are about learning how to navigate this discomfort in a way that produces better results for both the relationship and the business.**

Choose Your Mantra

How you start a difficult conversation will often determine the success of the rest of the conversation. So it helps to go into it with a mindset that serves you, not one that's working against you. To do that, you need to have a "mindset mantra" that will position you to have more confidence.

I once taught a difficult conversations workshop with the Women's Foodservice Forum in Buffalo, New York. During that event, we discussed what mindset mantras worked for various people. One woman raised her hand and said, "Choose discomfort over resentment." I love that! She reminded all of us that management requires us to choose short-term discomfort over long-term resentment.

My mindset mantra is, "Love people enough to tell them your truth." I learned this from a CEO who asked me, "What's the difference between loving someone versus enabling someone?" It took me two weeks to reflect on that question. I finally went back and shared with him my answer: "If my love ever gets in the way of you taking accountability for yourself, then that's not loving; that's enabling." Too many managers enable team members' behavior because they either don't have the difficult conversations, take too long to have them, or sugarcoat their message. I owe it to the person, our relationship, and the business to love them enough to tell them the truth as I see it.

Some of the other mindset mantras that people have shared in the past include:

- My reaction is my choice.
- Put the relationship first.
- I lead by example, even in tough talks.
- Don't confuse uncomfortable with incapable.
- Seek understanding, not victory.

- Embrace curiosity.
- I lead with empathy, not ego.
- I value resolution over winning.
- I choose to navigate this conversation with integrity.
- Difficult now. Easier later.
- I am responsible for my message, not their response.
- I approach all things with an open heart and a clear mind.
- Trust is a team sport.

Too many managers walk dreadfully into a difficult conversation thinking, *I don't want to do this. I can't believe I have to do this.* Or, *I just want to get this over with.* You deserve better for yourself, and the other person deserves better too. What is a mindset mantra that, if you could really buy into, would better serve you during the hard talks?

The Biggest Mistake in Difficult Conversations

The biggest mistake I often see managers make in difficult conversations is going into them not trying to learn but to mandate that someone change without understanding or caring about why the behavior happened. You'll never be able to shame or bully someone into changing their behavior. When managers don't make a difficult conversation feel like a team effort, people retreat to their separate corners, then each person becomes more focused on defending themselves. They stop listening and start judging, and all sense of "we're in this together" is lost.

Preparing for a Difficult Conversation

There might be some people who disagree with this, but I don't think you should spend a long time preparing for a difficult conversation. These conversations are important, and they deserve adequate preparation. Still, if you overprepare, you'll likely become so mechanical and rigid in the conversation that you won't be able to flex and pivot if needed.

There are four essential questions you need to answer before having a difficult conversation if you're the one who will initiate the discussion:

1. *What specific behavior do I want to discuss?* You don't get to unpack every grievance or problem you've ever had with that person over the course of the entire relationship. Get clear about the one or two core behaviors that are both recent and eroding the relationship or the other person's effectiveness.

2. *What is the impact of the behavior?* Explain why the actions being demonstrated are important. Highlight the impact, whether this is on the individual's growth, the effect on the team, the relationship between the two of you, their ability to form healthy relationships with their peers, or the impact on customers.

3. *What do I need to take accountability for?* Anytime a relationship breaks down, both people have a part to play. Those parts aren't always equal though. Get clear about any accountability you need to take during the conversation. Your ability to do this will often give others permission to do the same. Examples could be staying silent too long and not speaking up sooner, thinking the issue would resolve itself, not knowing how to address things, or not setting clear boundaries/expectations.

4. *What needs to happen to resolve the issue?* Part of the reason you're having a difficult conversation is so you can renegotiate the relationship and discuss what you need from each other. You're never going back to the same relationship again. That one is no longer working. Get clear

about what you think you need from the other person to move forward in a more productive, trusting way. Be open to adjusting this answer as you learn and discover more from the other person during the conversation.

Taking the S.T.E.A.M. out of the Conversation

At this point, you have your mindset mantra, and you've done adequate preparation. It's time to have the difficult conversation. The goal of every difficult conversation should be to approach the talk in a way so you can really listen and hear each other's experiences. To do that, you must focus on what you can control to take the STEAM out of the conversation.

Safety

Safety is the most essential, fundamental step in this difficult conversation model. Too many managers want to jump right into the "Truth" step and start with the problem they want to discuss. When you start with what you disagree on, you'll often end that way as well. Managers who build trust have a responsibility to first make the conversation safe. That's the only way people will be vulnerable, take real accountability, and be in a place to listen. This section of the model won't take long, but often it'll shape the outcome of the rest of the conversation. Think of it as putting your toe in the water to test it out versus cannonballing right into the chaos. You can use your presence to either put people on edge or at ease; those are your only two options. Managers who build trust put people at ease while still holding them accountable. That's leading with head and heart.

There are many ways to make a conversation safe: timing it well, picking a neutral location, managing your intensity, etc. However, the three primary actions I recommend for creating safety in a conversation are the following:

Start the conversation with what you agree on. What do you know to be true for you, the other person, or both of you? Don't make something up or say anything you don't believe. This should be vulnerable and authentic. For example:

- "I know moving up is important to you."
- "I know we're both committed to getting this project over the finish line."
- "You've always said we could come talk to you if we needed to."
- "It feels there's been tension in this relationship for some time, and we've been ignoring it."

Briefly highlight the issue, and make it feel like you're in this together. For example:

- "I saw some things in the meeting yesterday I think might hold you back, and I feel like I owe it to you to share those with you so we can get you where you want to go."
- "I've been struggling to understand what's needed from me and just wanted to get your perspective to make sure I'm adding the most value to the project."
- "It feels we have different ideas on the budget and staffing resources, and I want to take the time to understand things from your perspective."

Ask permission to have the conversation. We want people to psychologically buy into having the conversation. Therefore we end the "Safety" section of the model by asking permission to have the conversation with them. For example:

- "Would you be open to talking about this?"
- "Is this something we can discuss together?"
- "Can we talk through this together?"

I've never had someone say no to having a difficult conversation when I've opened this way, but if they did, I would honor their no without removing responsibility. The conversation doesn't have to be on my timeline. Now may not be a good time for them emotionally. That's fair. I want them to be in the best possible position to listen and share. So I might say, "I get that now is not a good time. When in the next few days can we meet?"

Truth

When the person says yes to engaging in the difficult conversation, you're ready to move into the "Truth" section of the model. This is where you'll leverage preparation questions #1 ("What specific behavior do I want to discuss?") and #2 ("What is the impact of the behavior?"). You'll clearly state the problem from your perspective and share why it matters. Don't talk too long here. You'll always have a chance to circle back and share more if needed. Don't overthink how to say it. Just be genuine. My rule is, "Be brief and be brilliant." Additionally, you're not responsible for how people take the message, but you are 100 percent responsible for how you deliver it. Make sure you're being both transparent and tactful.

If appropriate, you can also weave in your answer in preparation to question #3 ("What do I need to take accountability for?"). I often recommend ending this section from a place of curiosity where you ask the person, "So what's really going on?" "Can you help me understand?" or "What should I know?" Once you ask the question, be quiet and let them process what you just said. Your only job then is to quietly move into "Explore."

- *Example #1:* "The other day, when Sally tried to give you some feedback during our team meeting, you became very dismissive and rolled your eyes. It felt like you tried to shut her down with your intensity so the conversation would end. And it did. Frankly, I was taken back and surprised by your response. This is the first time I've seen this side of you, and I want to make sure it doesn't become the standard for how people on the team talk to each other. Help me understand what happened here."

- ***Example #2:*** "I've had a few employees share with me that they're struggling to work with you, so they've started to pull back. They often feel you don't want to collaborate because everything must be done your specific way. They say they try to offer suggestions, but they're always dismissed with reasons why it won't work. This obviously impacts the dynamic of our team, so I just wanted to share the feedback with you and see if you were even aware that this is the perception of a few others. What can you tell me?"

- ***Example #3:*** "Over the past few months, we've been discussing how important it is to follow the processes put in place. We've documented them, and you explained you understood them. However, over the past two weeks, clients weren't responded to within forty-eight hours, and I haven't been getting your reports by our agreed-upon deadlines. I find myself getting increasingly frustrated because I feel I've been patient and doing everything I know to make sure the expectations are clear, but the issue keeps happening. We simply can't keep moving forward like this. What's really going on?"

- ***Example #4:*** "First, I need to tell you I'm sorry. I feel I've been avoiding this conversation for too long because I didn't know how to bring it up. I care about this relationship, and I don't want to mess it up, so please forgive me for putting this off for so long. Someone recently told me that you went to my boss and shared with him that I was dropping the ball on the project and not communicating. If that's true, I'd like to understand your perspective, because I have a different one. I've wanted to believe that we have the type of relationship where we could come talk to each other first about things like this. So what is it I should know?"

Explore

This part of the model is where you stop and invite the other person to respond and share their truth. Exploring sounds like the easiest part of the model, but in fact it's the most difficult. Your only job is to be fully present and listen, but what will you do when you disagree with what they're saying, when they don't take responsibility, or when you feel attacked? Can you stay present and curious, listening to what they feel and the reasons why, knowing in advance that you'll get your chance to respond?

Acknowledge

You heard what they had to say. Now stop and acknowledge their perspective. If you jump in and immediately refute what was said or bypass everything you just heard, you'll often make it much harder for yourself through the rest of the conversation. Therefore acknowledge what the person shared. Remember: Acknowledgment doesn't mean agreement. It simply means you care enough to make sure you heard them correctly.

You have at least three ways to acknowledge what you just heard:

Validation statements. A simple statement to let someone know you heard them.

- "Thank you for sharing that with me. It helps me understand your perspective better."

- “I wasn't aware. Thank you for telling me.”
- “It's clear you've given this a lot of thought, and I respect your viewpoint.”

Empathetic statements. A statement where you acknowledge the emotion you think the person was feeling and why. I use this statement when someone is emotionally charged, and I want to dampen the intensity of the conversation. I learned early in my career that someone getting loud in a conversation is often a sign that they don't feel heard. It's then that I need to put empathy before more information. You'll know you did this tactic right when the person responds with a yes or nods their head in agreement. They're affirming that you see and hear them. They'll now be better positioned to hear what you're about to say next.

- “It's probably frustrating to keep giving your all when you feel others don't notice it.”
- “It must feel emotionally exhausting to keep talking about the same issue over and over.”
- “It can be infuriating to wait on others for simple tasks when you're trying to drive things over the finish line.”

Reflective Statements. This is a communication technique where you reflect back what you heard the other person say in your own words to ensure you're talking about the right thing. This technique will help prevent you from going down the rabbit hole with someone, talking about everything under the sun and not getting any resolution from any of them. Most people you'll speak to haven't even thought through the issue in that much depth until this conversation, so this tactic helps clarify what you're dealing with.

- “So the big concern for you is how to move up without coming on too strong?”

- "So from your perspective, you don't feel you need to communicate what days you're taking off?"
- "If I'm hearing you correctly, it sounds like you don't feel appreciated for the work you're doing."
- "So your bottom line is that people shouldn't take things too personally, and they should leave their feelings at home?"

This technique is a win-win regardless of what you say because the other person will either say yes and now you know you're on the same page, or they'll say no and explain their position in more detail.

I hope the model I just shared goes so easily for you that everyone's on the same page, takes instant accountability, and you can simply move right into the last step, "Mutual Agreements," where you talk about what you need from each other. The reality is usually quite different. Most difficult conversations will never be a linear process where you start at Safety and go straight to Mutual Agreements in one path. Gosh, I wish it were that easy! Generally, after Acknowledge, you'll go back to telling your truth some more, exploring their truth some more, acknowledging their thoughts some more, and around and around you'll go until you finally feel you're at a place to move forward. Only then can you move into Mutual Agreements.

Mutual Agreements
This is where you'll share your answer for preparation question #4 ("What needs to happen to resolve the issue?"). However, during the conversation, you might have learned more information, which changes what you think should happen moving forward. Great! Don't stay stuck to what you previously wrote. Give yourself permission to adjust as necessary.

Just remember, you're never going back to the same relationship again. That one wasn't working; that's why you needed to have a difficult conversation in the first place. So you'll want to spend time renegotiating the relationship and talking through what you need from each other differently moving forward. A few items you might consider discussing include:

- Specific actions you need from each moving forward
- Timeline of when things will happen
- Any resources or education needed to meet those new expectations
- The best way to follow up or give feedback moving forward

Finally, managers who build trust will take a moment at the end of the conversation and validate the person for engaging in the conversation with them. This is a sincere thank-you, and it reinforces the message that this is a relationship where people can talk about hard things together and leave in an even better place than before. That final thought might sound something like the following:

"Really quick . . . I wanted to say thank you again. I know these types of conversations aren't always easy or comfortable. I appreciate you trusting me enough to be honest, sharing your point of view, and giving me some things I need to think about as well. I thought this was a good and constructive talk."

As you can see, management requires you to engage in different conversations. This is why managers who build trust must be excellent communicators. No one is coming to you as their manager and telling you what type of conversation they need. You'll need to discern the type of conversations necessary to bring out their best. It will take practice. It will take some mess-ups. And it will require intentionality.

You've got this. I believe in you.

CHAPTER SUMMARY

- Managers who build trust must have the discernment to know which types of performance conversations they need to engage in with each employee.

Feedback Conversations

- Feedback is nothing more than me sharing information with you about what you're doing well or what you need to do differently so you can improve.
- Delivering useful feedback requires three primary factors:
  - Creating an environment of safety
  - Addressing specific behavior
  - Highlighting the impact of that behavior

Coaching Conversations

- Managers should engage in coaching conversations with employees when they don't know how to get from Point A to Point B.
- Coaching is not about giving people the answers or trying to "fix" them.
- The goal of coaching should be to get people thinking differently about the topic now, then understanding what needs to happen in the future.

Teaching and Mentoring Conversations

- In teaching and mentoring conversations, you are explicitly sharing what's worked for you based on past experiences.
- Managers should engage in mentoring conversations when they feel sharing their experience with a team member might close a knowledge gap and possibly provide a new way of doing things.

Difficult Conversations

- It's time for a difficult conversation when the issue at hand is significantly affecting the team or individual's performance, when it's clear that the problem won't resolve itself without intervention, and when the potential negative impact of not addressing the issue outweighs the discomfort of the conversation.
- Difficult conversations are about learning how to navigate this discomfort in a way that produces better results for both the relationship and the business.
- How you start a difficult conversation will often determine the success of the rest of the conversation.
- When managers don't make a difficult conversation feel like a team effort, people retreat to their separate corners, then each person becomes more focused on defending themselves.
- There are four essential questions you need to answer before having a difficult conversation:
    1. What specific behavior do I want to discuss?
    2. What is the impact of the behavior?
    3. What do I need to take accountability for?
    4. What needs to happen to resolve the issue?
- The goal of every difficult conversation should be to take the STEAM out of the conversation so we can really hear each other. This is the model for how to navigate these conversations effectively:
    - **S**afety
    - **T**ruth
    - **E**xplore
    - **A**cknowledge
    - **M**utual Agreements

SEVEN

Teams are only as
Good as your belief in them.
Always find the good!

PLAY 4:
RECOGNIZE WHAT'S RIGHT

One of my favorite quotes on the subject of recognition comes from Oprah, who said, "I would tell you that every single person you will ever meet shares that common desire. They want to know: 'Do you see me? Do you hear me? Does what I say mean anything to you?'"

Managers in every organization bear a unique responsibility to make others feel seen. **Recognition is the single most effective way to make people feel seen and valued.** Leaders in every organization should be held accountable for ensuring recognition becomes a habit, not an isolated incident that happens once every few months. If you know Gallup's twelve questions for driving employee engagement, you'll know their research recommends that employees receive some recognition or praise for doing good work every seven days. That can only happen if you have ongoing conversations with your team members. Most of the research I've read on recognition in the workplace highlights that most employees feel they don't receive enough recognition. I'm a big believer that most people gravitate to spaces where they feel seen. So if you don't recognize your talent, then someone else will come along and see them for who they are. You can't afford that. When recognition becomes a habit of all managers, it creates a ripple effect across the entire organization. You'll move from just managers recognizing employees to employees recognizing each other. Create a culture where your employees feel seen, and I promise that your customers will be seen as well. Everyone wins!

Years ago, I worked at Yum! Brands, known for their recognition culture. At the KFC headquarters in Louisville, Kentucky, each floor had recognition walls directly across from the elevators, highlighting their employees' efforts. Each month, a group of leaders would collect all the recognitions and decide who would earn the "culture hero" award. They would put together a makeshift "marching band" to play in the halls and alert everyone that a hero was about to be recognized. Then, they would surround the individual's desk and begin cheering. That associate would be given the culture hero trophy and the superhero cape and glasses for a picture. They would also be awarded a tricycle to ride around the office until another associate was named the next culture hero. Yum! Brands made recognition fun, and it was a consistent part of their culture.

Additionally, before team meetings, managers would send out notes to remind attendees to fill out a recognition card for anyone in the meeting they wanted to acknowledge. We'd start each meeting with these recognitions. At the end of the meeting, our manager would put all the recognitions in a bucket, then draw a random card and give a small gift card to the person recognized and the person who recognized them. This was a simple, easy way to reinforce their recognition culture.

Managers who build trust find meaningful moments every day to recognize and highlight individuals living the company culture, adding value to the organization and creating a better experience for the people they serve.

You'll know recognition is alive and thriving in your organization and your team when it's not just you leading the efforts but employees taking the initiative to recognize each other. Excellent management isn't about doing all the work. It's about strategically creating a space for the work to happen and then reinforcing it as often as possible.

Some best practices I learned from working in a recognition culture include:

- Connect all recognition to your company's core values.
- Deliver recognition promptly.
- Highlight the impact of an individual's efforts.

I often hear people debate whether recognition should be private or public, or big or small. **All recognition is meaningful, so don't overthink it.** Just start! I've never heard of an associate getting upset because a manager praised their efforts publicly. Conversely, I've never heard of anyone being offended because they received a thank-you note. If you can personalize recognition to the individual, even better!

At The Trust Architect Group, we have a personalized recognition form that we ask every team member and even our clients to complete if they feel comfortable. Our form is automated now, so it feeds directly into our online system. However, we started by having people complete a PDF form. The purpose of the form is to help leaders understand what people like so they can tailor their appreciation.

On our personalized recognition form, we ask for the individual's birthday, a brief description of their household (family, pets, etc.), and the best address on where to send them something if it's mailed. We then dive into their favorite things. Here is the list of favorite things we ask people to complete:

- Snacks
- Restaurants
- Ways you like to relax
- Cologne or perfume
- Things you can't get enough of
- Causes/Charities
- Places to shop
- Hobbies/Interests
- Most useful gift certificates

We knew a client loved Tiffany perfume, so after a large event, we had the perfume waiting for her when she arrived home. Another person had a personal connection with the Make-a-Wish Foundation, so we made a donation in her honor. One of my team members loves TJ Maxx and Sephora, so I'm able to get a gift card for the things she values. Another person loves sour candy, so for Halloween, I had a large delivery of sour candy sent to her. None of these recognitions cost a lot, but they made a really big impact on the individuals who received them.

Finally, large recognition gifts are fabulous, but they're often not scalable or able to be given frequently. Please don't discount the power of small but meaningful recognitions. They pack a really big punch. Each manager should be held accountable for recognizing people, and the best organizations have a strategic process that makes recognition consistent throughout the company.

Find the Good

Steven Abigail is one of the best leaders I've met at implementing recognition. He explained to me that when he was a manager and leading people both in the United States and overseas, he was taught to look for mistakes and then correct them. He emphasized that there's a time and a place for that, but "if all you do is look for the bad, you're going to find it." Your team is going to become exhausted, and you'll never bring out the best in your people. It's just as important that you make a habit of finding the good in your people. When you look for the good, you'll always find it as well. Steven challenges himself and his team to catch people doing what's right on a daily basis. Sometimes, that recognition comes in the form of a face-to-face thank-you, public acknowledgment within the company's newsletter, a compliment inside the team's WhatsApp group, or on social media. He believes any form of recognition must be timely, specific, and sincere. Steven also explained that what gets recognized gets repeated; therefore performance becomes more consistent, and the team's culture improves.

Steven and his leadership team aren't waiting to learn everything about the individual before they recognize them. They start where they are with the tools they already have. They also understand that it's important to recognize both the individual and the entire team.

Here are fifteen good ways you can recognize individuals on your team:

- Provide a verbal or written thank-you.
- Spotlight an employee on social media.
- Share recognition with leaders higher up in the company.
- Give a paid day or afternoon off.
- Pay for a home service of their choice.
- Provide a gift card for one of their favorite places.
- Bestow a personalized recognition award.
- Invest in someone's professional development.
- Celebrate the person's achievements outside work.

- Leave small gifts or treats on someone's desk.
- Pay for a one-year magazine subscription.
- Provide LinkedIn recommendations.
- Send a care package.
- Post a recognition video from the CEO.
- Nominate them for an industry or trade award.

And here are ten good ways you can recognize your entire team:

- Host a small party to celebrate the completion of a project or milestone.
- Create a visible recognition wall where you post achievements.
- Provide a pop-up breakfast, and do some quick group shout-outs.
- Hand out company merchandise, and take a team picture.
- Bring out a local food truck for a fun lunch break.
- Order some personalized team gear they can wear or use.
- Provide a car wash voucher to each team member.
- Bring in a masseur for chair massages throughout the workday.
- Post team pictures on LinkedIn and spotlight their efforts.
- Plan a fun team outing (for example, a *Chopped*-style cooking competition).

I recently heard Jamie Lee Curtis on the *Today* show talking about why she puts out so much positivity in the world. She explained that she feels life is hard for everybody. Everyone has a lot of stuff going on, and no one is immune to the hardships of life. She feels that if you're really in communication with people, you let them know how much you appreciate them. That's what recognition is! Sometimes, it's being someone's hype person as they win a big award, like Jamie was for Michelle Yeoh during the Oscars. Other times, it's just a simple thank-you and letting someone know you believe in them. "Not enough people get support," Curtis said. Jamie understands she can use her presence to change that for the people in her world. As a manager, you have the chance every day to make the people around you feel supported. Make your presence count!

Managers who build trust understand that recognition isn't manipulating people into doing what they want. It's a genuine act of appreciation to let people know you see them, and that what they do matters. Honoring each team member's efforts fuels their trust and engagement. Team-wide recognition fortifies a sense of unity and belonging. This dual approach around recognition allows you to bring out the best of the collective group.

People need you to see them. Recognize what's right.

CHAPTER SUMMARY

- Managers in every organization bear a unique responsibility to make others feel seen.
- Recognition is the single most effective way to make people feel seen and valued.
- Recognition must be a habit, not an isolated incident.
- Most employees feel they don't receive enough recognition.
- You'll know recognition is alive and thriving in your organization and on your team when it's not just you leading the efforts, but employees taking the initiative to recognize each other as well.
- Managers who build trust find meaningful moments to recognize and highlight individuals living the company culture, adding value to the organization and creating a better experience for the people they serve.
- All recognition is meaningful, so don't overthink it.
- Don't discount the power of small but meaningful recognitions.
- It's important to recognize both the individual and the entire team.
- Recognition is not manipulation to get people to do what you want.
- By honoring each team member's efforts, you fuel their trust and engagement.

EIGHT

Your humanity
Is your greatest gift and it
Brings out people's best.

FINAL THOUGHTS

Managers change lives - for better or for worse. We can all think of managers who believed in us, held us accountable, and gave us the coaching and opportunities we needed to continue moving up. We can also instantly recall those managers who didn't invest in our relationship, took advantage of our time and trust, and didn't set us up for success. Both made an impact. The type of impact was very different though!

Great management isn't a personality trait; it's a practiced skill. It's learned through experience and intentional development, and it's reinforced through accountability and genuine recognition. Being a manager who builds trust is about being brilliant at the plays that we know work if you want to bring out the best in others. It's about consistently showing up, building authentic relationships, setting clear expectations, leaning into performance conversations, and recognizing what's right. If you do that, you're going to make a big impact. But the responsibility is not only on you. Your team members have a responsibility to show up as well. You can pour all your belief in them and give them the tools, feedback, and recognition they need to grow, but it's up to them to decide if they're willing to make the same investment into the relationship with you and the organization. If they're not, then you need to discuss whether your organization is the right place for them.

Here's the truth for all you managers who build trust: you are going to mess up from time to time. You don't always get it right as a parent or a romantic partner, and the same will be true for how you lead others. Please, be able to acknowledge your mess-ups, learn from them, and use those lessons to make you an even better leader.

Come back to this book when you're struggling in a relationship with one of your team members. Remember, this is your playbook to use as things come up. Go to the pages that address your problem, and see what ideas you can leverage to take the next right step in the relationship.

Above all else, hold on to your humanity. You will face challenges on your management journey that aren't easy, and you will even question if you're being "punked" because things feel so ridiculous. These challenges can easily make you want to harden up, become judgmental, and tempt you to lead from only your head-space. This exact behavior disconnects us from ourselves and the people we serve, and it prevents us from making the high impact we say we want to make.

You were always meant to offer more: more love, more understanding, more accountability, more opportunities, more trust, and more impact. That's the power of your presence. Please never forget who you are.

I said it earlier in the book, and I'll repeat it here: As a manager who builds trust, you're so much more than just a manager. You are a catalyst for change, an architect of culture, and a champion of people and performance. This is your legacy, and you will change people and spaces for the better.

And if no one tells you they believe in you, I believe in you.

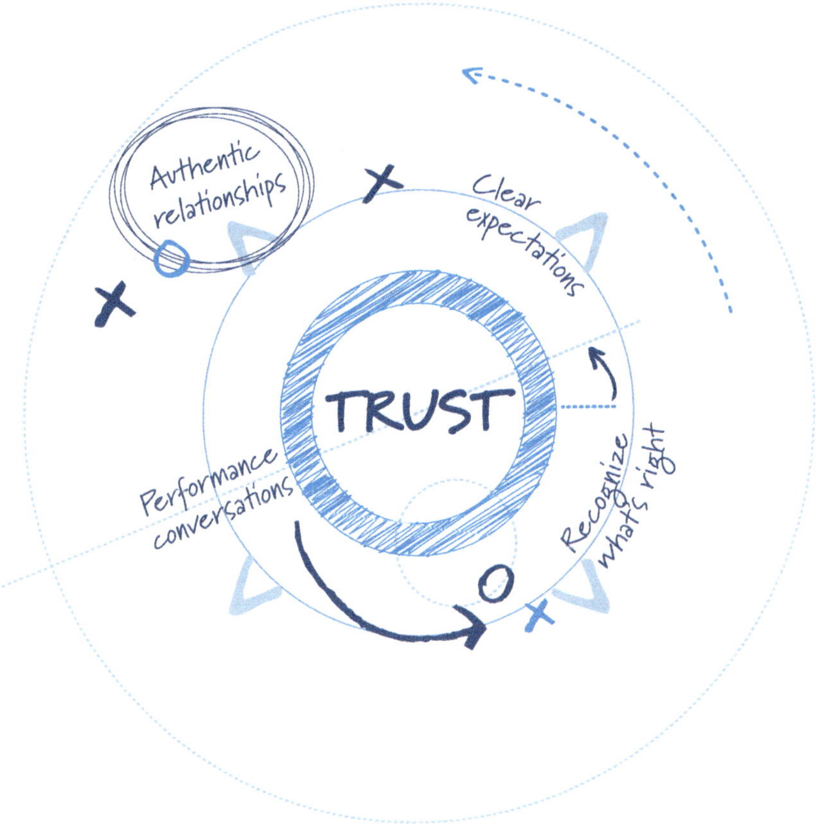
Authentic relationships
Clear expectations
TRUST
Performance conversations
Recognize what's right

TRUST MANIFESTO

Managers who build trust don't just hope for, wish for, or think about trust. They build it. They take decisive action and use each move as a playbook for the type of trust they want to experience in their relationships. To them, trust is not a touchy-feely concept. It's the currency of every relationship, and it decides whether people come back or not.

The following manifesto is our collective call to action for leaders to deliberately build the kinds of relationships and communities that bring out the best in themselves and others.

+ JOIN US!

In a world that can sometimes feel dark and where people feel disconnected, we, the Trust Architects, emerge as a beacon of hope.

Our singular mission: to rekindle meaningful relationships through the power of trust where people feel safe, seen, and valued.

We believe in a simple yet profound truth—that trust is the key to unlocking a world where people feel they belong and keeps them coming back for more.

Our journey is one of transformation, guided by the unwavering conviction that trust can bridge the vast distances of disconnection, and radically change how we lead, love, and communicate.

To us, building trust is more than a mission; it's a movement.

A movement toward a society where trust is woven into the fabric of every interaction, and communities are built on the foundation of transparency, tact, and togetherness.

These principles are mirrored in our approach to leadership, which, to us, is an act of presence.

Building a trust-centric world isn't easy. Trust requires courage and resilience. It requires us to consistently choose love over fear, discomfort over silence, empathy over judgement, accountability over enabling, and a commitment to always hold onto our humanity.

We invite you to join us, to become architects of a world where trust is the foundation, and where people have each other's back.

Together, through each act of trust we demonstrate, we change people and spaces for the better. And in doing so, we light up the world by the difference we make in our families, communities, and organizations.

We are trust architects.

ABOUT JUSTIN PATTON

If you want your leaders to think differently about trust and how they communicate, Justin is your person!

As the founder of The Trust Architect Group, Justin Patton works with leaders on how to build communities of trust inside their organizations. He is an award-winning author of multiple books, and he has expertise in communication, leadership presence, and how to build a culture of trust that keeps bringing people back for more.

Justin has received the highest earned designation from the National Speakers Association, is a credentialed coach with the International Coach Federation, and is part of the prestigious Forbes Coaches Council.

WANT MORE LEADERSHIP INSIGHTS?

EXPLORE ALL OF JUSTIN'S BOOKS AT JUSTINPATTON.COM/BOOKS OR ON AMAZON

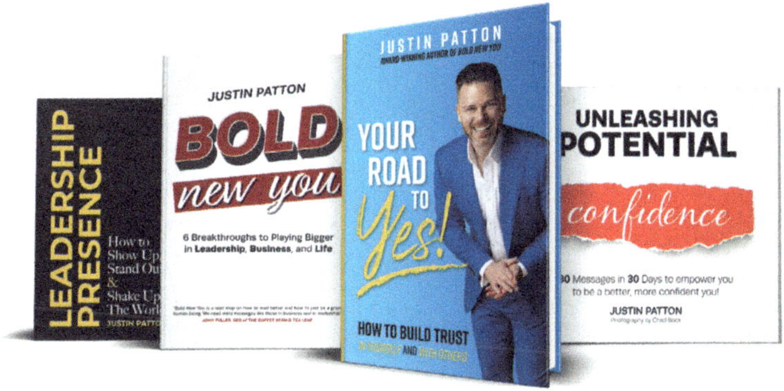

YOUR ROAD TO YES!

Dive into the science of building trust with yourself and others.

BOLD NEW YOU

Learn how to get out of your own way and be a better leader of yourself.

LEADERSHIP PRESENCE

Think differently about how you show up with these actionable strategies.

UNLEASHING POTENTIAL

Cultivate stronger confidence with this 30-day self-guided workbook.

Made in the USA
Las Vegas, NV
18 November 2025

34679651R00066